ONLY
IN
AMERICA

A POETIC LOOK AT THE
STATE OF OUR NATION

HARGIS R. SALEEM

authorHOUSE

AuthorHouse™
1663 Liberty Drive
Bloomington, IN 47403
www.authorhouse.com
Phone: 833-262-8899

Published by AuthorHouse 12/28/2023

ISBN: 979-8-8230-1971-2 (sc)
ISBN: 979-8-8230-1970-5 (e)

Library of Congress Control Number: 2023924446

Print information available on the last page.

Any people depicted in stock imagery provided by Getty Images are models,
and such images are being used for illustrative purposes only.
Certain stock imagery © Getty Images.

This book is printed on acid-free paper.

ONLY IN AMERICA

(a poetic look at the state of our Nation)

(explicit content)

SUPREME COURT DECISIONS

POLITICAL CIVIL WAR

CONGRESSIONAL RETRIBUTION

MASS GUN KILLINGS *(no solution)*

HOMELESSNESS

OATH TAKEN

NOT

THE INDICTMENTS OF A FORMAL PRESIDENT

GOP FIGHT FOR POWER IN CONGRESS

***Evil has taken control*

Hargis R. Saleem

CONTENTS

IN THIS BOOK

In this book of poems, you will find true events and the time when they unfolded.

You will come to understand that freedom in America does not always mean you are free. You will see how evil has infected the (so called) leadership of this Country through deceit, lies, and trickery.

And his efforts to destroy the very foundation of the Democracy that governs this land. You will, also, see how hypocrisy and greed have DE-valued the human life and have allowed schools, churches, night clubs, parades, and City streets to be unsafe.

This book of poems is a continuation of my first book (America do you see what I see?). But because there are forces that are trying to rewrite and or destroy true history, this will enlighten the youth and remind the ages of days gone by.

This book of poems is about corruption on the highest level. It is an account on how our election system has being constantly attacked by those who have been made to feel and believe that every vote should not count (depending on who you are voting for).

In this book of poems, you will see how the rich and the Political powerful have put forth efforts to exercise revenge and retribution on those who disagree with their policies and thought process.

In this book of poems, you will come to see and understand the demise of the mentality that other Countries once respected, feared, and looked to for leadership. When you have Priest, Preachers, and teachers raping children and a United States President and Congressmen not living up to their oath, the world views that as weakness.

There are some crimes (mentally, physically, and spiritually) that happens ...

ONLY IN AMERICA

MY EDUCATION

My education, I get from the streets … from the things I see and the people I meet.

My education, I get when I turn on the tub … and hear talk about the real bad dudes (you know the rapists, the Priests, and the Politicians).

I get my education when black State Reps. Are expelled from the House of Tennessee because they attend to the cry of the people for justice.

I get my education when AR-15's are use to kill people in schools, churchsh, night clubs, and super markets.

I get my education when the rich and powerful feel that they are above the law and their resources make some people say they didn't see what they saw.

I get my education when laws are changed (by men) to take away a woman's right to decide what she can or can not do with her own body.

I get my education when 'black history' is not allowed to be taught in schools because the slave master's children get offended about the truth.

I get my education when black people are beaten and gunned down(by the police) in the streets or in their homes and they and the grand jury feel that it was justified.

I get my education when parents fear sending their children to school not knowing if they will return back home.

I get my education when men who want to be women and women who want to be men are politically fazed out of theirs human rights.

I get my education when thousands of people are sleeping on the streets because cash money is the 'God' of this world.

I get my education when free speech is used to spread hatred, racism, and death.

Yes, I have a degree like no other ... and my oath is to keep informing my sisters and my brothers. This degree didn't come from tap-dancing or playing ball and can't be hung on my walls. It doesn't matter if you march or pray, it can't be washed away.

Yes, I get my education from the streets ... from the things I see and the people I meet.

Hargis
4/8/23

I GREW UP IN A TIME ...

I grew up in a time ...when there was some value to a penny and a dime
        and you listened when grown folks talked,
I, also, grew up in a place ... where emphasis was placed on race
        and you stepped aside when white people walked.
There were certain places I couldn't eat ... drink water or take a leak
        because society labeled me 'colored' not black,
we had 'used' school supplies ... use books that told me (about myself) lies
        and my family lived in run down houses filled with rats.

I grew up in a time ... if you were arrested for a crime
        that you did not do,
they would lock you up ... and didn't give a fuck
        that's when time walked and never flew.
I grew up playing in the streets ... and you ate what was fixed for you to eat
        or you didn't eat at all,
lets not get this misunderstood ... the food at home was damned good
        because girls learned how to cook before they even could crawl.

I grew up in a time ... when there were pure minds
        when men were real men,
they did what they could ... because their word was good
        and hugging and kissing on another man was a sin.
During that time ... you didn't (openly) cross that line
        because you knew where you stood,
but times have now changed ... and many of our so-called leaders are deranged
        now early death is a good possibility in my hood.

I grew up in a time ... that help mold and shape my mind
        that made me the person that I am today,

*I didn't dis respect my father or my mother … my sisters or others
and to my God, every night, I would pray.*

Yes, I grew up in a time … when I was allowed to grow up in time.

Hargis
5/16/23

I WRITE

Everyone has a calling … some teach school and some are good at balling
some fight for human rights … all I do is write.

I write about the sunset and the sunrise …
I write about little breasted woman and those with big thighs.

I write about things that are good and things that are bad …
I write about the education or mis-education in our Country that are making
people mad.

I WRITE

I write about slavery and the injustice of today …
I write about (so called) leaders, all they want us to do is pray.

I write about the Democrats, the Republicans, and the Supreme Court too …
I write about this Government and how they won't do anything for me and you.

I WRITE

I write about the mass shootings and all the drive – by (s) …
I write about the hurt of the families, because all they can do is cry.

I write about the racism and hatred that man has for man …
I write about the starvation and homeless people all across this rich land.

I write about people making money off of other people's suffering and pain …
I write about children disrespecting their parents, and say that the parents are
the blame.

I WRITE

I write about marriages and relationships that go bad …
I write about communication outside of sex they never had.

I write about how the drugs in the streets are no different than the drugs
*   you get in the stores …*
I write about how a lot of these drugs are turning some women into
*   home and street whores.*

I write about the evil in our country that is spreading pretty fast …
I write about how some friends want you as friends, but want you to kiss their ass.

I write about the laws of this Country that we should obey …
I write about how same sex marriage has become normal today.

I write about how illegal drugs have become legal in most States …
I write about a former President inspiring people to practice hate.

I WRITE
I WRITE …
AND WILL CONTINUE TO WRITE

Hargis
9/3/22

"FOR REAL"

It can flow forever
but the flames of the earth will dry up your tears
then you will find yourself running into the deserts
trying to drench your thirst for some reality with the sands of life
but realizing that all of this madness
comes from the minds of men.
Also, realizing that after spending the youthful years of your life
under the direction of those who society calls parents ...
you haven't even been born.
Yet everyone expect for you to understand why suicide was committed.
Is death the only way to bring life into existence??
The courts didn't understand that "HOLLIE" wood
determines the faith of millions
because time doesn't wait on anyone
and age is just a thought process ...
life is understandably short, yet still they feed us commercials
every chance they get and watch us choke with the 'desire' to have
because our educational system has been distorted
causing the earth, that fertilizes the seeds of tomorrow, to burn
with the desire to be real.
The way we process our thoughts ... our solutions will only bring
about more problems because there is no such thing as "great men"
but if you free your mind ... your ass will follow.

Hargis
6/11/79

ONLY IN AMERICA

All over the world the same thing … the shootings in America has not changed
       two hundred and eighty eight people have died this year,
in Texas today, an eighteen years old … killed his grandmother, then he locked and loaded
       went to an elementary school that was near.

Nineteen children and two adults … this shooter didn't give a fuck
       no one knew his reason or why,
they were from six to ten year old … his story has to be told
       like what education did he have to cause little children to die.

In Buffalo … a week ago … ten people were killed in a grocery store
       an eighteen year old drove two hundred miles to kill blacks,
we all know about the tragedies in this land … and know that racism and shooting go hand in hand
       but nothing is never done about it (and that's a fact).

The making and selling of guns is a multimillion dollar stroke … politicians cater to NRA because their money is like dope
       making the lives of the people an after thought,
some Congressman won't say a word … to help the people they (suppose) to serve
       or pass any laws to get the killings to halt.

The NRA is hosting an event this week … Ted Cruz, Trump, and the boys will be there to meet
       to line their pockets with more cash,
the agenda is not known … to them, 'gun control' is wrong
       the participants will do nothing but kiss NRA ass.

Hargis
5/24/22

GUNS
(THE SAME OLD SHIT)

Another shooting, another shooting … in Ok, Az, and Chattanooga
        still Congress won't work together hand in hand,
Republicans won't talk about guns … don't want to loose those NRA funds
        unless it's about distributing more guns though out this land.

Biden is talking about raising the age … that doesn't take guns from the center
stage
        teenagers aren't the only ones pulling the triggers,
pressure in life is great … putting everyone's lives at stake
        making 'red necks' thinking they are justified in killing niggers.

The Senate won't even bring gun control up … unless Biden is willing to kiss
Trump's butt
        the American people are confused as hell,
how some Senators got to DC … it's hard to see
        most of them should be in jail.

Even though the Democrats are in charge … they are not pushing real hard
        for other votes to win,
more people will be killed … by racist or the mentally ill
        then families and the Country will grieve once again.

Something has to be done … it can't be more guns
        because the only consequences to the shooter is death,
this will go on and on … and will become a popular song
        because those that rule are controlled by wealth.

In the last two weeks … mass shooting has reached a new peak
        young folks have got their feet on the gas,
making it hard to go anywhere … because these shooters don't care
        about children in school or the people who wear the badge.

The Republicans and the Democrats are both full of shit ... they won their election, then flipped the switch

> *they are surly not listening to what the people say,*

America has become the true wild, wild west ... when it cones to mass killing, she is the best

> *and all the people can do is pray.*

__THERE SHOULD BE NO COST FOR HUMAN LIFE__

Hargis
6/5/22

THE ONES WE CHOOSE
(BE MINDFUL)

Mid-term election is here again ... Politicians are in the community calling us friends
        trying hard to get us to vote,
telling us the same old lies ... about when, where, how, and why
        filling our heads with political hopes.

Talking about issue after issue ... wanting us to elect him or her to that position
        to represent us and the State,
but don't be miss-led ... because it's all about that bread
        they will be trying to 'fill up' their financial plate.

'We, the people' don't understand ... how we can elect a poor man
        that use to get bait on credit, just to fish,
he goes to DC ... representing you and me
        four years later, he is super rich.

Now he us telling us what our goals are ... cause he is now a political super star
        his agenda is now in order,
the man who use to fish in our creek ... now has a Senate seat
        and now his loyalty is to the party.

He can be be recalled ... like fruit, vegetables, and alcohol
        if 'we, the people' so will,
it's not an easy task ... cause now he's got all that cash
        and we all know that money will cause some thoughts to be killed.

We have to vote for what we really, really believe ... so we won't be deceived
        by Billy Bob, Johnny, or Mary Sue,
and make sure the 'promise' to us they keep ... and please don't fall asleep
        because that money will make them forget about me and you.

Hargis
6/13/22

NO MONEY ... NO RIGHTS

Cadillac(s), Mercedes, Limousines ... expensive wine, the American dream
       the rich party day and night,
around the corner and two blocks away ... an eviction notice, the family can't stay
       no money ... no rights.

In the ER, two have been shot ... one has money, the other has not
       equal services (sometimes things get kind of tight)
one is placed in a room ... the other died at noon
       no money ... no rights.

The world in which we live ... everything is for real
       money and race are in control
the homeless population is getting big ... because jobs that pays money has a tight lid
       so in most cities, their rights is a financial load.

       No money ... no rights

The electricity is off ... a bad storm is the fault
       everything is shut down,
some communities have to wait ... while the power board deliberate
       about money and race in what part of town.

       No money ... no rights

I know this seems odd ... because every man and woman is equal in the eye sight of God
       but humanity on earth is another thing,
your abilities and your skills ... determine if you die or live
       money to the poor is just a dream.

       No money ... no rights

People march in the streets … after someone has been beat
and their 'rights' to breath have been taken away,
the marching don't last … because the city pays cash
that's how the organized leaders earn their pay.

No money … no rights

The poor live in the worst part of town … the City (for a few bucks) will tare it down
up rooting the homeless and the poor,
moving them so the tourist can't see … the reality of the real C-I-T-Y
but there is always a promise to do more … but

No money … no rights

This poem you may or may not like …
some of you may have some knowledge and some insight … and
some may think that you have to fight for human rights …

but in America

No money … no rights

Hargis
7/23/22

ONLY IN AMERICA
(PART TWO)

Evil is in the air ... it is blowing sin everywhere
  making right look wrong and wrong look right,
women walk around half naked with no shame ... children are getting shot at close range
  and 'deranged minds' are walking the streets (armed) day and night.

Men are allowed to marry men ... that used to be a sin
  I guess America is the modern day Babylon,
a kid can buy a gun with just an 'ID' ... and take a life then walk away free
  but Congress makes no rulings about guns.

Everyday our safety is at risk all across this Nation ... at church, night clubs, schools, super markets, and train stations
  because evil has a grip on every State,
politicians, preachers, prostitutes, and pimps ... none (I mean none) are exempted
  so they make it sounds like everything is great.

War and destruction is the world we live in ... we do unto others as we do our friends
  because everyone is afraid to get involved,
so little babies and children die ... because we won't challenge the lie
  so most crimes in America never get solved.

There used to be a time when you didn't see ... commercials for alcohol and cigarettes on TV
  now growing, selling, and smoking weed is legal in most States,
romanticizing HIV ... and showing 'he' kissing 'he'
  and on computers is where most are finding their mates.

Hargis
5/27/22

REVELATION
(THE BEAST)

It's two thousand and twenty two...evil is showing what it can do
　　dis-spite the many cries for peace,
Asia, Europe, and Africa the same...death and destruction can not be
contained
　　Russia is killing and will not cease.

For those who believe in the book...'revelation' describes how the beast
looks
　　and the marks on his forehead and in his hands,
if you got some wisdom, this beast you can't miss...his number is 666
　　and the book say "for it's the number of a man".

I'm not a preacher of religion...God and you, that's your decision
　　but evil is embedded in the mentality of those who rule,
lets not get it twisted...and lets keep it realisty
　　because confusion, lies, and deceit are the tools that evil use.

If you look back over the last fifty years...you will see how evil slowly
appeared
　　it took away morality, humanity, and taste,
then it stripped you naked with no shame...by giving you money and
fame
　　then it took away your logic and your faith.

Now a man like Trump can just walk in and take control...
through lies and deceit, destroying 'will power and souls'
　　to him, laws of humanity do not apply,
he will never accept the truth or defeat...so he create diversions and
turn up the heat
　　because he understands that evil will never die.

So take some time...and dig deep into your mind
      to find out who you are on this planet earth,
step up to the plate...it's not too late
      to display what God put in you at birth.

Hargis
3/8/22

HOMELESSNESS
(WHO DO THEY GIVE THANKS TO)

It's turkey time ... basing the meat and drinking wine
        thinking about the homeless people and the cold weather,
some families will hug, laugh, and smile ... doing what they do family style
        while the homeless can only hope and huddle together.

On the tube, they want money for holocaust survivors, children, and dogs
nothing for the homeless who's life has stalled
        America has more billionaires than any other country on this earth,
on the tube they target the poor ... to give more
        because they care about the human worth.

Some of it just the hustle and a game ... playing on human emotions to
satisfy over looking their pain
        for less than one dollar a day,
what people have to understand ... is the nature of the hustling man
        they are coming at you in many ways.

So many sleep in the streets ... sometimes with nothing to eat
        but they were once a part of somebody's household,
there are shelters that will take in many ... but out in the streets there are plenty
        and in the winter, some will not make it in the cold.

City administrators everywhere ... are always on the news talking about how
much they care
        for the man, the woman, and the child,
but the homeless population grow ... because the administration is moving too
slow
        so they blame it on 'red tapes' and 'files' and always say "it will take
        a while".

There is an education that was missed ... to cause the homeless situation to exist
        the questions are what and why?

Being broke in a money rich land … is hard on a jobless woman and a jobless man
but millions are spent on new homes while homeless people in the
streets die.

Homelessness is nothing new … without money this could happen to me and you
because success in this country is measured by cash,
I don't know what happened to mans' humanity … but homelessness is a reality
and the population is still growing fast.

"may the peace and blessings of God be upon them"

Hargis
11/23/22

"PEEPING"

America, America land of the free … home to brave and heaven for the U-G-L-Y
    and still we say it's the greatest Country there is,
we have more billionaires here than any other spot … and more killings and rapes
that seem to never stop
    the whole Country is dressed in fear.

They are paying billions for military while jobs go away … the homeless
numbers are
increasing in every City every day
    while the inter City lands are controlled by gangs and fights,
children are growing up in one state of mind … get what you can get, don't worry
about the crime
    humanity is just a whisper in the night.

Technology is out of control … it's waging war in the minds of the young and
the old
    people are made consumers from birth to death,
commercials got something for your ass … from breast cancer to gas
    and insurance companies are paying very little for your health.

There is a lot of gun fire in schools … some City Officials are acting a fool
    some want to be a woman, tired of being a man,
more and more are coming out … even those with some "NBA" clout
    what has happened to our educational system across this land?

It is said that in America, everything goes … for the right amount of money you
can turn NUN(s) into ho (s)
    everyone is under pressure to get that cash,
America is all about money … Capitalism is not funny
    and without it, your life will not last.

*Peeping in America, all you can do is pray ... because all kinds of shit is
happening in this day*
*   yes, America is truly the home of the free,*
but you have to watch how you talk ... and where you walk
*   because America is also the home and heaven of the U-G-L-Y.*

"JUSTIFICATIONS"

Justification is a game within itself ...
>   it over rules 'your right' and it will destroy your health.
Justifying an increase in rent to see what the renters will bare ...
>   is like justifying the firing of millions because the 'profits' aren't there.

Justifying a killing because of the uniform ...
>   is like justifying the up rooting of black communities and see no harm.
Justifying a religion to enslave a people's mind ...
>   is like justifying community prisons because of the increase in crime.

Slavery was justified and so was the killing of Emit Till ...
>   too many black babies are being born, justification for the birth control pill.
Preparation for war is what it seem ...
>   justification for the destruction of the American dream.

Justifying 'this' just to justify 'that' ...
>   is like justifying white by justifying black.
Justifying being rich by justifying the poor ...
>   is like justifying a pimp by justifying the whore.

Justifying the bad conditions that people are in ...
>   is like justifying a lie just to justify sin.

Hargis
2/15/87

AMERICA
LOVE IT OR LEAVE IT

Mass shooting almost everyday ... nothing is being done to take guns away
      so people will continue to die,
Democrats and Republicans argue and fight ... over voting and human rights
      and all families can do is protest and cry.

America is evolving back into her mentality of the past ... when they shoot
first and ask questions last
      but nothing has changed for black folks,
we are still getting killed ... it seems at will
      in homes, in church, and with the police knee on our throat.

A black man was stopped ... but he feared cops
      so he ran because an arrest he was trying to avoid,
he was shot 45 times ... then hand cuffed with his hands behind
      but the Grand Jury said the police will not be charged.

It's only in America where these stories are told ... because it's only
in America where mass shootings are out of control
      and evil is spreading fear everywhere,
now you can get guns at a young age ... no back ground checks even if your
mind is filled with rage
      Republicans and NRA don't care.

You see, God in America is money ... so for the rich, their days are always sunny
      and the poor is used as servants and for games,
there will be no gun laws or deals ... it doesn't matter how many people are killed
      the rich will always say "the poor is the blame".

Lets not get this wrong ... because it's the same old song
      how the city official's thoughts and prayers go out to the families that
      grieves,

but it's just for that moment in time ... they are always on television lying
thinking this bullshit is what the public needs.

So our safety in America is at risk ... in church, in schools, at the mall, or
at home taking a piss
     because hatred and guns go hand in hand,
Congress won't stop the sale of guns ... because they will loose NRA funds
     so death by shooting has become normal all across this land.

AMERICA ... LOVE IT OR LEAVE IT
(BY PLANE OR IN A GRAVE)
IT'S UP TO YOU

Hargis
5/6/23

WE, THE PEOPLE
(A STATE OF DARKNESS)

Republicans are still doing what they do ... trying to deny people rights like me
and you
>   their goal is dictatorship,
Trump is the root cause ... he controls the 'party' that has no balls
>   democracy (in part) they are trying to rip.

The Supreme Court is their last play ... to get all 50 States to do it their way
>   so that the evil can set up its' happy home,
we, the people have got to fight hard ... to keep America from becoming dark
>   but we can't do it by marching and singing songs.

All of this started back in the garden of Eve ... when women did shit you
wouldn't believe
>   to get men to go against Gods' will,
Trump was there ... convincing people that God was not fair
>   then he signed 'the kill Jesus' deal.

Now he wants control ... of the voters and the polls
>   so he is creating confusion and disgust,
by having the blind lead the blind ... as he keep lying
>   but his main target is 'just us'.

All he doesn't kill, he put in jail ... with years of hard labor and no bail
>   and it can be for any little thing,
like having dogs fight ... or speaking out for human right
>   or for preaching about having a 'Dream'.

In America, we the people, need to understand ... the mentality that control
this land
>   that is pulling us apart,

we the people, will be the only ones that will bleed … if we allow them to succeed then the State of America will truly be dark.

Hargis
7/6/22

PUT UP OR SHUT UP

A lot of people are surprised ... that the January 6th Trial is still alive
    it's been almost three years,
over 900 people have been charged ... but the main organizers are still at large
    and they don't have any fears.

Trump said that if he is re-elected in 2024 ... he will use his authority and let them all go
    including the ones that caused bodily harm,
the Quans and the Oath Keepers said they were armed and ready to do what ever it takes ...
to stop the 2020 election certification (the old fashion way).
    All because Trump sounded the (stop the steal) alarm.

Many have come forth to tell what they know ... how Trump tried to give our Democracy a knock out blow
    he said he couldn't count on Mike P.
so they marched down to Capitol Hill ... doing Trump's will
    but Trump went back to the 'House' to watch it on TV.

He was asked by his daughter ... and others
    to call this insurrection off,
in order to survive ... Congressmen and women had to run and hide
    now the whole world knows that Trump is just a mob boss.

They interviewed Ginni T. for four hours ... about how she tried to keep Trump in power
    her e – mails to Mark M. proved it,
when she took the stand ... she said she never told her Hus...Band
    but the Committee and the American people know that was just 'bull shit'.

*The Committee keep stalling and changing the date ... but they know that the
American people are tired of the wait*
      they need to indict Trump or shut it down,
kiss him on his ass ... and suck in his gas
        go to Mar — A -Lago and give him his crown.

                               Hargis
                              9/30/22

THE FIGHT
(OF THE PEOPLE / FOR THE PEOPLE)

The midterms elections have come and gone ... the Republicans are wondering
what went wrong
     a lot of their people lost
they all thought that Trump ... would get them over the hump
     you know the conspiracy boss.

The Senate they didn't win ... the Democrats are in charge again
     but the 'House' they did take,
when and where did America go wrong ... she used to be politically strong
     but now all the politicians are filled with revenge and hate.

The Republicans are filled with sin ... talking about revenge
     wants to impeach Biden and bring his son to trial,
they want to go after everyone that Trump don't like ... bring out the ugly in
people and take away some of their rights
     their message is very clear and loud.

About America, lets be real ... people with power have had Presidents shot and
killed
     because they didn't like their directions,
trying to bring stability and peace ... and the hatred for one another to cease
     and trying to establish some unity and affections.

So here we are in 2022 ... you have to choose between the red or the blue
     the politically 'crips' and 'bloods' gangs,
the DOJ seems to be afraid to make a move ... against an (evil former) President
who has broken all the rules
     and have no fear or shame.

Some people in the party are trying to split ... they are tied of Trump bullshit
     they are looking for a brand new face,

but the 'mob — boss still has his hands on their throats … trying to kill any
political hope
        to stop his 2024 Presidential race.

Trump should be in jail … get fucked by men with no bail
        until he understands,
that America is 'of the people and for the people'
        and don't cater to any one man.

Hargis
11/27/22

CIVIL WAR
AMERICA'S STRUGGLE FROM WITHIN

America is at war within herself ... waged by those with political power and
wealth
       trying to put democracy to bed,
they are trying to control ... the young and the old
       by ripping 'human rights' to shreds.

The Republican Party is moving State by State ... changing laws through fear
and hate
       not caring about the people's will,
evil still sits on the throne ... the Republican Party is his home
       and he doesn't have a problem ordering people to kill.

Distraction, confusion, and rage ... is evil's stage
       because he wants everyone to see,
his power ... in these dark hours
       and want you to be whatever he wants you to be.

Mass shooting is still in affect ... because Congress won't or hasn't done
anything yet
       but give shouts to the families that grieves,
States are making it easier to get killing machines ... that put them in the hands
of the deranged and those that are mean
       evil is a mentality that our society feeds.

A 'civil war' is where we are today ... Republicans against Demarcates, both
not caring what the people say
       because it's all about power and money,
children will continue to die ... and families will continue to cry
       but our days will get darker before they get sunny.

There are those who say ... at least in public anyway
        that the best is yet to come,
the best what ... guns, funeral homes, or human rights getting fucked
        or the best way to teach our children to run.

This is a message of great alarm ... for those who read or hear this poem
        because 'justice' and 'democracy' in America is just about dead,
we (in our own way)have to fight ... for human rights
        and force evil out of our heads.

Hargis
4/13/23

THE GREATNESS OF AMERICA
(NO ONE IS ABOVE THE LAW)

In America, nothing has really changed … everybody is still running the same
old games
       it seems like the mind set has stopped,
nothing has been done … to stop the selling of guns
       so shooters are still killing a lot.

Trump is on trial … the GOP is going wild
       trying to defend all of his wrongs,
they still have his fear … and are still kissing his rear
       while Trump keep singing the same old (I've done nothing) song.

Most of his lawyers have quit … cause they are tired of his shit
       and because he never take their advise,
he thinks he knows it all … acting like a Mob boss
       and he thinks his lies will suffice.

He has been twice impeached and twice indicted … still red necks and racists
think he is mighty
       and they think that he 'should' be above the law,
he makes up his own rules, because he is afraid to lose
       but everything he says is false.

Fox news is always on his side … and keep telling their viewers lies
       about what they think they are hearing and seeing,
they are pointing fingers at the judge and the DA … because they are doing
what the law say
       in order to make "America great again".

Trump says if he goes to jail .., violence in America will be hell
and that he has his people standing by,
but in America, dictators don't rule ... and through elections, the people choose
and the will of the people ain't shy and we will answer his cry.

Hargis
6/15/23

STILL WE RISE
(THE SUPREME COURT RULING)

*The Supreme Court has done it again ... taking away some privileges from the
people with dark skin
        I'm talking the affirmative action rules,
with today's vote of 6 to 3 ... higher education might not be
        available to some blacks in some schools.*

*With the ruling today ... the Supreme Court did say
        that the 'color of the skin' should not be a consideration,
this, also, applies in the work place ... where you are hired and or fired because
of your race
        it like: not eating because of inflation.*

*They want to stop teaching black history ... in some of the States in the Southern
District
        because the slave master children don't understand,
they want to rewrite the story ... to give them more glory
        and continue the degradation of the black man.*

*They can't stop the prophecy from coming true ... through out history they
thought they knew
        how to keep the children of God down,
the devil (for thousands of years) has kept up the fight ... to make right seems
wrong and wrong seems right
        to make sure that 'no one' was heavenly bound.*

*In the black homes, they took the fathers away ... the killed and continue to
kill the young
black men of today
        but still we rise,
they took away our language, our religion, and our names ... gave us their
identity and used us for their sports and games
        but still we rise.*

The Supreme decision … in trying to stop our vision
*   is just a bump in the road,*
the presence of GOD is here … this, the devil does fear
*   but we rise, so that the truth can be told.*

Know ye the truth and the truth will set you free
*   and 'we the people' need to be free*

Hargis
6/29/23

THE HUSTLE IN THE HOOD
(2024 ELECTION YEAR)

2024 election is gearing up ... Politicians will be in the hood trying to suck
     out of us our votes,
they have taken control of women birth, our schools, and our money ... they
determine
how and where we live, what we eat, and what days will be sunny
     while always talking about our future hopes.

The Politicians in every City and in every State ... are constantly in political
debates
     about the homeless situation,
they, also, promise jobs they have not ... and their love for the people who just
got shot
     and how they will reduce the high cost of inflation.

This will go on for another year ... most will have their token blacks standing
there to cheer
     with their signs held up high,
saying "blacks are for this man ... because he is the only one that unite this land
     and he understands the people's cry".

Joe Blow and Mary Sue ... they may or may not be new
     at hustling in the hood,
but they are knocking on our doors ... telling lies to us like the ones that came
before
     and they all say "I would if only I could".

We listen to them talk that talk ... but very few are able to walk that walk
     but we always choose, who we're gonna choose,
some Politicians are for real ... but they all have those political skills
     like con-men and street hustlers, who think they can never loose.

At the end of the day ... Politicians treat us as their prey
        pointing fingers at others saying they are the blame,
some Politicians want to be dictators ... but has become creators
        of misinformation and have no shame.

Those that are currently in charge ... have no strong hearts
        and they are always misunderstood,
but when their political minds ... need to be refined
        they always come to practice on hustling in the hood.

Hargis
7/5/23

WHAT WAS HIS OATH??

Trump is trying in every way ... to delay, to delay, to delay
    the trials of his indictments,
because he thinks he can win ... the White House again
    without the people's consent.

All of his appeals ... and his crooked deals
    have all been denied,
voters are still sending him a lot of cash ... Fox News host, Hannity, is still kissing his ass
    even though they know that he is full of lies.

He promised in January 2017 ... to protect the Constitution and the American dream
    he said this in front of the American people and God,
but soon, many found out ... what he was all about
    and was not fit to have the Commander in Chief job.

Some are talking about pardoning this man ... who has really fucked up this land
    because he wants the power of a dictator,
he thinks that the American people are fools ... so he is trying to change the rules
    under the pretends of making America greater.

His state of mind has been exposed ... and his indictments grows
    he is fighting for his life any and every way he can,
Trump is an 'ass hole', and can only produce shit ... but he vowed to never quit
    but he doesn't understand that the Constitution and Democracy Govern
    this land.

Hargis
7/21/23

EYES OF THE WORLD
(IS WATCHING)

*The world is waiting for the results of the US events ... to see what will happen
to the twice impeached and twice indicted formal President
       to determine if democracy has any value at all,
if the DOJ ... has it's way
       we are talking about jail time this fall.*

*We have already been told ... that the DOJ is close
       for the last two years,
Trump is fucking with their mind ... by pro-longing trial time
       while still issuing out fear.*

*He doesn't have a plan ... for the people of this land
       except to retaliate against those he doesn't like,
and to free those in jail ... who on Jan. 6th (for him) raised hell
       trying to over throw the peoples' rights.*

*World leaders are shaking their head ... and saying it looks like freedom in
America is dead
       and China now has become the king,
while Politicians are fighting each other on Capitol Hill ... Russia is still
killing people at will
       immigrants are wondering 'what ever happened to the American Dream'?*

*The GOP is saying that President Biden is too soft and too weak ... and can't
stand too long on his feet
       and he need to be replaced,
but if Trump is their choice ... the American people will not have a voice
       and there will be an open war between the races.*

*The NATO Countries are at a loss ... because America use to be the boss
       and the out spoken leader of the free world,*

but the GOP is trying their best ... to put that 'title' to rest
    I'm talking about the Republican boys and girls.

They are sticking with Trump which is kind of sad ... because he is the worst
and the most criminal minded President that we ever had
    and he only cares about himself,
racists and red necks love the ground on which he walks ... will travel hundreds
of miles just to hear him talk
    and (to him) they will give up their wealth.

History will remember him as the Presidential G. O. A. T. ... the con-man
who destroyed the people's hopes
    to enjoy and live in a good economical and safe environment,
with a strong and powerful love ... for the God up above
    but lets not forget that from down below, Trump was sent.

"NOW THIS"

Everything and everybody that he touches turn to shit ...
this man with the orange hair, you can't miss ...
the 'bible' says his number is 666 ...
he is powerful and he is rich ...
and you do not want to be on his shit list.

He got Putin To invade Ukraine ... after they said no to his Presidential game
    to find some dirt on the family of Joe B.,
now he is attacking all the D A(s) ... that have come forth to say
    that he should not be free
because of all of his crimes ... and all of his lying
    trying to over throw Americas' democracy.

Now he is running for the House again ... trying publicly to destroy those who
are not his friends
    while eliminating the other candidate,

he had four years to work … but all he did was dig up dirt
and brought forth and promoted nothing but hate.

THE EYES OF THE WORLD
(IS WATCHING)

Hargis
7/7/23

CONGRESSIONAL SHAME
(2023)

The Government shut down got a break ... because McCarthy and some Democrats voted late
     to extend the dead line for a few more weeks,
Matt Gaetz is up in arms ... saying the Speaker has caused the GOP some harm
     so he is threatening to take away the Speakers' seat.

Today they brought forth the pros and the cons ... but in the end Gaetz and his people won
     McCarthy can no longer be,
some GOP are visibly upset ... because they are not sure of the effect
     of the first 'voted out' speaker in history.

After receiving the Speakers' seat ... nine months later, he faced defeat
     because of the promises he made,
he didn't keep his word ... so Gaetz and others say he doesn't deserve to serve
     because lying is like a two edge blade.

Matt Gaetz seem to now be in charge ... Trumps' new boy with no heart
     will the GOP bullshit ever cease?
their internal fight is great ... putting life in this Country at stake
     the new Speaker Gaetz, Jordan, or Scalise?

Sitting on their dying bed ... they are still trying to put into our heads
     that the Democrats are the blame,
so, here we are today ... the GOP is trying to figure out a way
     to deal with and hide their Congressional shame.

Hargis
10/4/23

A LEGACY OF DECEIT AND LIES

When you turn on the T V ... you can't help from seeing the indictments and
trials of Donald T
     from fraud to insurrection,
he has threatened the judges, witness, and the DA (s) ... saying "if you come
after me, I'll make you pay
     while asking his fans to send money to show their affection.

This fraud case is all about his past ... and how he lied about the value of his
properties to rake in millions of cash
     then brag about what a great business man he is,
his whole organization is about to go down ... he is sitting in court with nothing
but a frown
     Donald T has never faced anything this real.

After two and one half days ... Trump left New York and went on his way
     back to his home in the South,
he realize that he is about to loose a big part of his game ... he is calling this
trial an American shame
     because he might have to give up his money, his hotels, his golf course,
     and his Florida house.

He is asking his fans ... to send money (if you can)
     even if it's just one dollar,
to off set these costs ... so he can still be the boss
     and to stand by for more info to follow.

Between now and the month of May ... more serious trials are on their way
     and he may end up doing some jail time,
his cry will still be "I haven't done nothing wrong" ... Marjorie Taylor Green
and Matt
Gaetz will still carry on
     his legacy of deceit and lying.

This Country will be in for a shock … if his Presidential run is not stopped
    because he and his followers think that he is and should be above the law
    (it seems),
Fox News and most of the GOP are defending his rights … to lie, cheat, and
steal and to keep up his fight
    to put America in a position 'that we have never seen'.

Hargis
10/5/23

AMERICA ... AMERICA

America, America the home of many States ...
      with polluted air and chemical made food
and still you brag about being great.
Your dollar has fallen ... and your leadership is stalling
      hypocrisy is openly displayed,
products made here ... consumers have some fear
      because most workers are only paid minimum wage.

Your Politicians think they are slick ... but the 'Feds' put them in a trick
      exposing some corruption on Capitol Hill,
but since it was Congress that got exposed ... the masters of loop holes
      the matter is now being killed.
And within your States ... is one big unit of hate
      because racism is celebrated and toasted,
so children grow old ... after having been told
      that they are better or worse than most.

America, America so brave, so strong, so right
      you have infected the earth ... but what makes matter worse
is that you look at it and say "oh what a sight".

Your technology is good ... but let it be understood
      that it's not always used that way,
your deceit and lying ... and international spying
      will come back to bite you in your ass some day.

America, America the land of the brave ...
      your people are yearning to be free,
to enjoy your good ... which is misunderstood
      from sea to shinning sea.

Hargis
4/12/80

THE TRIAL OF THE CENTURY
(LIBERTY OR DEATH)

The January 6th insurrection trial is on TV … so that everyone can see
>   *how Trump tried to stop the process,*
of the certification of votes … and the peoples hope
>   *and putting Mike Pence to an illegal test.*

Some of Trumps' people are stepping up to the plate … testifying about Trumps' plans and the fake
>   *information about the election,*
still some Senators and Fox news are calling it a lie … even though 6 people did die
>   *while Trump watched it at the White House after giving out directions.*

Fox news (everyday) is singing their song … about how everything that President Biden do is wrong
>   *from the border to inflation to the high price of food,*
his meeting with the Jews and the Muslims and his support to Ukraine … they say he is insane
>   *and he is not fit to rule.*

Trump is the one that brought forth this pain … the hatred, the virus, the war in Ukraine
>   *because he wants to rule forever,*
his slogan is me, me, me … he wants to change everything he see
>   *because (like I said before), Trump is the devil.*

This trial is being telecast … we don't know how long it is going to last
>   *but the DOJ need to put him in jail,*
in America, this is all new … but my warning to you
>   *if Trump is re-elected, he will spit out holy hell.*

Hargis
7/16/22

WHAT ARE YOU GOING TO DO ABOUT IT?

The investigation of Trump was stalled for a minute … even though the
evidence against him is plenty
   his appointed judge said 'no' to the FBI,
the DOJ filed an appeal … then the shit got real
   the 11ᵗʰ District Court asked the judge why?
did she hand a judgment with no proof … Trump and his lawyers hit the roof
   because now indictments are on the way,
Trump said he did nothing wrong … you know his same old song
   but he is not dealing with the 'old' DOJ.

In New York, they got him for tax, property, and insurance fraud … his family,
his accountant, and his organization (they got them all)
   causing Fox news and some Republicans to shout,
the New York DA …want them to pay
   and all of his business (in New York) they want them out.

The January 6ᵗʰ committee … want him indicted for what happened in DC
   for trying to change the 2020 election results,
he and some others said that it wasn't true … but television showed it all to me
and you
   now some Republicans are telling him that he is 'fucked'.

In Georgia, they got him on tape … trying to convince the election officials of
the State
   to find him 11,000 more votes,
he knew it was wrong … you know his same old song
   but he thought that he had Georgia by the throat.

In Florida, the FBI conducted a raid … he is now saying it was staged
   and that the FBI planted the shit,
but his Special Masters … turned out to be his disaster
   and told him and his lawyers to 'prove it'.

Now Trump is on Fox news ... singing the blues
       saying he DE-classified all those files in his mind and by the wave of
       his hand
he was the President of the USA ... he is authorized to do things his own way
       which proved that he really don't give a shit about the laws of this land.

He, also, warned the Country at large ... that if he is indicted, this Country
will be torn apart
       he told his people to stand by,
he think that he can't be touch ... by the FBI, the DOJ, and such
       so it's okay for him to commit crimes and lie.

This has been going on for some time ... no charges, no fines
       the Criminal Hall of Fame has his crime list,
there are people who are trying to fight ... to make it right
       but to the DOJ and the FBI (what are you going to do about it??).

Hargis
9/25/22

"EVERYTHING GOES"
IF YOU ARE RICH AND POWERFUL

All over America, there is mass shootings and home invasions …
human trafficking and starvation
        but the Capitalist is making a mint,
you got judges and their families living in fear … by a crime boss who say his
people love him so dear
        the same guy, his property, to blacks he wouldn't rent.

Children just got killed in a school … by a gun toting fools
        confused, didn't know if he was a woman or a man,
this other dude who use to play ball … got tired of it all
        shot up the bank … cause it's common in this land.

Two black State Representatives got reinstated … the Republicans in that State
hate it
        but that was the people's will,
they have become known as the Tennessee three … but nothing happened to
whitey
        she said that her skin color was her special skill.

Trump got problems everywhere … but he doesn't care
        because he thinks that he has the right to be above the law,
in a Fox News interview, he was still lying … about how some people in court
was crying
        but no one but himself could see what he saw.

It has been reported that Supreme Court Justice Clarence T. …has been cheating
on you and me
        for over twenty years,
he has been receiving gifts worth millions … from his friends who is worth billions
        to this day, Clarence T. has no fears.

He said that there is nothing on the books ... that says he was wrong about what he took
      over this long period of time,
these things have been nice ... for him and his wife
      but you know what they say, for the rich and powerful, justice is blind
      (really blind)

                                                              Hargis
                                                              4/15/23

POLITICIANS
(SOME SAY)

This is the season ... when Politicians will give us all kind of reasons
        to vote for them next year,
some Politicians are talking good ... about cleaning up the hoods
        by taking away the violence and the fear.

Some Politicians say for our vote ... we won't be broke
        because the cost of living won't be so high,
they will regulate food, drugs, and gas ... the same lies they told in the past
        and will protect the schools, so that our children won't die.

Some Politicians put the blame ... on the war in Ukraine
        and the current administration,
some Politicians say they will bring about order ... and clean up the boarder
        and fix our China relation.

Some Politicians are still talking about the so-call steal ... which we know was not real
        but they know solid campaign plans,
what that is all about ... is to distract our thoughts
        to vote for or against the other man.

Some Politicians talk about guns and killings ... but none of them are willing
        to take on the NRA,
raising the buying limit of the age ... won't stop the rage
        Politicians just don't want to loose that pay.

Some Politicians talk about the homeless in the streets ... that have no place to sleep
        they have no money, no jobs, and very little ambitions,
they have no where to go ... and their numbers grow
        but the Politicians are the blame for their condition.

Some Politicians talk about unfunding the police ...because they are not at peace
      with the communities they are paid to protect,
some police are shooting ... some are looting
      some are kneeing on the peoples' necks.

Politicians ain't no jokes ... they don't represent the folks
      that voted them in,
some Politician tell us the same old lies ... and think they are wise
      but they all are filled with sin.

It doesn't matter if they are Democrats, Republicans, or No Label ... mentally
retarded, or disabled
      they know that the American people are looking for a new day
some Politicians do their best ... to put us at rest
      Politicians are crooked, there is nothing else to say.

"we the people must be free"

Hargis
6/19/23

A NEW DIRECTION
(IS IN NEED)

The Republican Party is upset ... over the Speaker's deal with the spending
ceiling debt
     now they are talking about taking away his job,
most of them don't really care ... about the American peoples' well fare
     or if they become homeless or starve.
The GOP and Fox News are trying hard to make President Biden look bad ...
forgetting about Trump (the worse President we have ever had)
     even though Fox News has been sued twice for spreading lies,
still they are doing what they do ... after firing one of their crew
     which came as a surprise.

America is falling apart ... because some leaders don't have it in their hearts
     and don't care about the people they are suppose to serve,
some of their minds are set on self ... and the possibility of wealth
     but all they are doing is us shit that is 'obscured'.

Some of the GOP are nasty and mean ... like that bitch name Green
     who wants to be Trumps' Vice,
but the breaking news ... is that Trump will not be the one that people will choose
     that means Trump will loose his run for the House twice.

Americans as a whole should be on a new mission ... and vote in 2024 for new
Politicians
     because most of the ones now ain't worth shit,
the 2024 voting solution ... should be called: 'the Politicians revolution'
     so we can throw that yesterday mentality in the ditch.

There are a few who really care ... our thoughts and ideals that try to share
     but their voices can't be heard,
the GOP have always shown their skills ... remember what happened in
Nashville
     again, we were looking at shit that was 'obscured'.

Those that understand should step up to the plate ... Democrats and Republicans
should have a serious debate
　　　not for an election, but what needs to be done,
to change the Country's direction ... to bring about more love and affection
　　　and to safe guard the people from guns.

Hargis
6/21/23

DONALD J.'S INDICTMENT (FINALLY)

Donald J. finally got indicted … everyone was excited
      as he called for his people to protest,
but there wasn't too many there … for his moment in history to share
      so the drama king was at his unusual best.

Miss Taylor Green came … but the New Yorkers put her to shame
      so she jumped back on her bus and moved on,
in New York, they don't play … plus this wasn't a good day
      that's why most of Donald J. people stayed home.

The first President to get impeached two times … the first former President
to get indicted for a crime
      some Republicans are backing away,
Donald J. keep saying the same old thang … blaming others for his childless
games
      but he never thought he would see this day.

The Republican Party and Fox News … are breaking all kinds of rules
      trying to keep him out of jail,
they are blaming everything and everybody they can … from the FBI to the
weather man
      from the White House to the person who delivers the mail.

Donald J. always say "I've done nothing wrong" … thirty four counts, he need
to change his tone
      he's hoping that the jury will set him free,
but there is no Bill Barr around … to block the path which he is bound
      or to take away the jail house key.

This is really a historical moment in time ... the first formal President indicted for a crime
paying for pussy with campaign funds ... right before his 2016 President run.

Hargis
4/4/23

STILL SOME CAN'T OR REFUSE TO SEE

It's October 2023 … still some can't or refuse to see
    the struggle and suffering of many,
in a Country that is suppose to lead … but is filled with hypocrisy and greed
    and have the resources that are plenty.

Freedom comes with a large price tag … who, when, why, and what decisions
sometime make the people mad
    the Supreme Court and a few others have sent this Country in reverse,
living in America is tight … only the rich and the powerful have all the rights
    the poor and the unfortunate can only cry and ride behind the hearse.

Child labor and sex slavery is on the rise … day care centers and churches are
used for drugs to hide
    because 'money' in America will set you free,
no money (no gas, no lights) … no money (no food, no rights)
    still some can't or refuse to see.

The GOP is answering the calls … of Trump orders because they have no balls
    he wants retribution against everyone he doesn't like,
so Jordan, Green, and Gaetz … who are extensions of Trump's hate
    are using their positions to keep up his fight.

This month in Georgia, the trials begin … of 19 women and men
    for conspiring to try to change the results of that State election,
some say they were doing their job … representing the President, who think
he had been robbed
    but his recorded phone call is used as his confession.

in Alabama, the Supreme Court said to redraw the voting zones … but Alabama
said "leave my niggas alone"
    they don't need a Representative,
so the struggle continue through out the State … bringing back memories of

George Wallace and his hate
        giving them more incentives.

This is the beginning of 2024 election year … and the GOP do have some fears
        so they are trying their best to eliminate or control the black votes,
because when you look at the hood … things are not that good
        but retribution is not a part of their hope
        STILL SOME CAN'T OR REFUSE TO SEE

Hargis
10/1/23

THE HIGH COST OF CRIME

In stores, a free for all ... has been installed
     even though there have been a few arrests,
store's new rules and polices are wild ... chasing the robbers is not allowed
     all the workers can do is watch and clean up the mess.

These crimes are happening in most States ... the store owner's livelihood is at stake
     and their video cams are little help,
the Mayors and the Governors don't know what to do ...the police rosters are few
     the economy of the city is hard felt.

Stabbing and fighting still exist ...walking from place to place, you are taking a risk
     kidnappers and rapers are still doing their thing,
there is no visible efforts or solutions ...Politicians have all but destroyed the Constitution
     and they are working hard to remove the American dream.

Drive (s) and mass shootings are everywhere ... the people in Congress don't seem to care
     unless it's one of their own,
it doesn't matter where you live ... or how many protests you give
     you are not safe (not even in your home).

Thousands are crossing the broader everyday ... seeking a safe place to stay
     sleeping in tents and on the streets,
filled with fear and confusion ... about the American illusion
     and the dream of freedom they seek.

Racism in America is openly displayed ... hatred for one another has boiled to a rage
     and any little thing can cause your death,

like a jealous spouse … or no love in the house
     or you can't afford the medications for good health.

"When leaders lie … people die"
     this is why… the cost of crime is high.

Hargis
10/6/23

"HAVE YOU SEEN?"

Have you seen ...
>
> *the brother who calls himself a priest*
> *who preach and preach, but practice it the least.*

Have you seen ...
>
> *the long lines of people looking for a job*
> *and the millions in this country that we know will starve.*

Have you seen ...
>
> *the 'ugly' that strolls through the streets at will*
> *ejecting fear into the community, always looking to kill.*

Have you seen ...
>
> *the homeless ... their numbers are growing fast*
> *no shelters, no food because our society worship "cash".*

Have you seen ...
>
> *the children who haven't had time to grow*
> *they're just babies having babies with no directions to go.*

Have you seem ...
>
> *the drugs they are pouring into our streets*
> *young kids are looking old, adults have that look of defeat.*

Have you seen ...
>
> *the break up of our family all across this land*
> *mothers not teaching their children and fathers not being the man.*

Have you seen ...
>
> *the same sex marriage, approved in many States*
> *where are the principles of Christianity and those who claim*
> *to have faith?*

Have you seen ...
>   *the destruction of the people minds and their wills*
>   *those who have made <u>money</u> their God, and for it they will kill.*

Have you seen ...
>   *the disappointment of hope*
>   *on the face of our people because they didn't vote.*

Have you seen ...
>   *the education of our people?*

Have you seen ...
>   *the education of our people?*

Have you seen ...

Have you??

Hargis
6/16/09

THOUGHTS FOR TODAY
(9/23/23)

Election time is here … people are living in fear
*   not sure what the future holds,*
gun violence is on the rise … politicians are still telling lies
*   and some are trying to change how the story is told.*

Money is tight … some are trying to kill voting rights
*   because they don't believe 'justice for all',*
Congress is fighting among themselves … trying to keep a former President
out of jail
*   now they want to bring the Country to a crawl.*

The evil in Congress is running wild … destruction from some is shouted out loud
*   they care nothing about the American people,*
McCarthy, Jordan, Gaetz, and Green … are trying hard to kill the peoples'
dream
*   they should be called 'the grand weepers'.*

Drug dealers are pushing drugs everywhere … a baby died from drugs in a day
care
*   they used this center as a drug undercover,*
people don't understand … the mentality of a drug man
*   this poison, they will sell to their mother.*

Voting out some of these Politician out should be our goal … for our health,
our well being, and our soul
*   if not, America (as we know it) will no longer be,*
our future generations will have no choice … because they will have no voice
*   and the true history of America they will not be able to see.*

Don't get it wrong ... America (today) is still strong
     but destruction is on its way,
this election ... may give evil an erection
     and allow him to fuck our democracy until it fades away.

Hargis
9/23/23

THEY ARE STILL TRYING TO MAKE THE LIE THE TRUTH

America is not safe … for your religious belief or your race
        so what is Democracy?
there are those who are trying to control the peoples' votes … by squeezing
freedom by the throat
        then there is hypocrisy.

Crooks, lairs, thieves, and pimps … their mentality, they are trying to implement
        power and more power are their goals,
Politicians are in charge … these animals have no hearts
        this Country they have stole.

Too many of us have old ideals and little hope … so without asking for anything,
we vote
        for the party that has always been a family tradition,
not caring what they do or say … and in those positions, too many years they stay
        they seem to be accepted under any condition.

Look at M. T. Green … the Georgia's hate queen
        she wants to shut the Government down,
on the Hill, she seems to be making all of the calls … because Kevin don't have
any balls
        and without her permission, he doesn't make a sound.

Nothing has been done about guns and killings … nor about the bum rushing
of business and stealing
        the House GOP is trying to save Donald T,
from trail Judges and DA (s) … the Black ones anyway
        and the world is waiting to see.

There have been earth quacks, floods, fires, and unbelievable rains …through
what most are calling 'climate change'
        tens of thousands have died,

here in America, the GOP don't seem to be concerned ...because they are trying
to get Donald T another White House turn
by continuing to spread all of his lies.

Hargis
9/13/23

IN PLAIN SIGHT
(A CON MAN AND A PIMP)

It's August of 2023 … and most of the GOP won't agree
        that Trump should or should not be indicted,
but three times he has been called to the well … and he is lucky that he is not
in jail
        now the whole world is somewhat excited.

They want to know if America is real … and if the lie is true about the steal
        that Trump ego refuse to let go,
he still has a few cronies … that is still chewing on that baloney
        but most don't represent the people any mo.

Is Trump the big American crook? … will he be let off the hook?
        Will Democracy be lost?,
these questions have been asked time and time … and how long will the GOP
keep kissing his behind?
        Or will America give honor to the crime boss?

Trump has raised over 200 hundred million since leaving DC … now the GOP
PAC has donated 40 million to for his legal fee
        a con man is always a con man everyday,
don't get it wrong … Trump's grip is strong
        and he is pimping his base in every way.

He may or may not do any time … for all or some of his crimes
        but he won't be the President again,
he will cry the blues … on why Biden didn't loose
        and give reasons why the system wouldn't let him win.

Then, maybe, the GOP will get hip … and develop some new leadership
        and get back to helping the people they represent,
they need to look at the reality … and get rid of the old mentality,
        and understand the propose to DC in which they were sent.

There will always be someone that's piss ... who will challenge why Democracy
exist

>   *because he or she wants the power to be,*

Trump wasn't the first ... nor was he the worst

>   *America, America is loved from sea to shinning sea.*

Hargis
8/7/23

"ONCE WE SEE AND UNDERSTAND"

Trumps' appointed judge gave him some time ... to keep spreading his conspiracy
theories and keep up his lying
    in hope he can win the GOP nominee,
Trump is doing a victory dance ... and convincing his fans
    thinking that 'his' judge has set him free.

He got other indictments on the way ... so he hopes and pray
    that he can hold them off until December of next year,
thinking that he is loved by most ... and wanting to get all of their votes
    then he can unleash (on those he doesn't like) unspeakable fear.

Some GOP are in shock ... to vote him, they say they will not
    saying that he is not fit to be in charge,
what is really wild ... some GOP (on TV)talk that shit and smile
    but their actions indicate that they have no heart.

Since taking over the House ... the Speaker (Kevin M.) has turned into a mouse
    and the GOP agenda has been Trump, Trump, Trump
the Country has not benefited at all ... Fox News and the GOP are too busy
trying to cut off President Biden's balls
    while driving millions of their supporters into the dump.

Trump is trying to win his case through the press ... by saying that the DOJ
and the DA (s) are causing a political unrest
    orchestrated by the President of the United States,
he keep saying that has done nothing wrong ... but trying to over throw the
Government and he had classified documents found in his home
    and the hiring of the voter over seers that were fake.

Jack Smith mind is clear and free ... so are the DA (s)in Fl.,Ga., NY, and DC
    so will Trump end up in jail??,
if so, America will not be the same ... all of his supporters will be looking for
some one to blame

they will all cry that the 'system' has failed.

2024 will be the worse year ever … because of the GOP support of the devil
     who will bring 'fire' from sea to shinning sea,
some will get sun tans and grow dreads … some, from the shock, will become
mentally dead
     most, who are now Representatives will no longer be.

Once we see and understand the lie … almighty God will put out the 'fire'
     and bring about unity and peace,
you see, only God is able … to cause minds to be stable
     he, also, can cause confusion to cease.

"ALL PRAISES ARE DUE TO GOD"

Hargis
7/25/23

RUDY G.
(TO SING OR NOT TO SING)

Rudy G, once a very powerful DA of New York City ... has now become
an ass kissing ex-lawyer, doing the devil bidding
      telling lies about the 2020 Presidential election,
he was down in Georgia trying to kill hope ... talking about he seen the dead
in line casting votes
      now he wants to make a full confession.

"The devil made me do it", he wanted to say ... but the raft of Trump will make
him plead the 5th all day
      unless the Government agree,
to give him special considerations ... so he won't loose his relation
      ship with others and to keep him jail free.

Jack Smith said okay ... but you have to do it my way
      and you just can't lie,
in your grand jury interview ... you have to tell all the shit and when you knew
      or you will give prison a try.

So Rudy G. said he will sing like Luther ... and crow like a proud rooster
      telling all he know,
but the devil has a long reach ... and threaten to snatch from his head that bleach
      to remind Rudy that he is his 'ho'.

Now the American people are waiting to see ... what will happen to Rudy G.
      will he keep his promise to Jack,
or will he just give in ... to the master of sin
      who has taken the spinal cord out of his back.

Rudy is broke, they say ... he was found guilty for trying to force two elector
to see things his way
      so now he is struggling to get that cash,

he looked to Trump for some help … Trump said I've my own problems, help
yourself
    and by the way, Rudy, kiss my ass.

Hargis
6/29/23

GOP TRYING TO HOLD ON

The DOJ has got Trump's ass in a sling ... cause the people all around him are
beginning to sing
       about how crooked he really is,
all of his lawyers come and go ... mainly because they can't take any 'mo'
       of Trump trying to enforce fears.

The DOJ tried to give him a little lead way ... but Trump would not stay
       in line with the courts' rules,
the GOP got him thinking that he is a king ... so he thinks he can do anything
       but all he ever done was loose.

Now he is asking Congress to intervene ...to try to stop this trial before it convenes
       but all of his bullshit has surfer-ed to the top,
some GOP members are backing away ... they no longer believe anything that
Trump say
       because the evidence that Jack Smith has is a lot.

His former lawyers say that Trump should give in ...and take the plea offer with
a grin
       and he won't get any jail time,
but Trump is playing it hard ... because he has 'his appointed judge' in charge
       and she will not let in most of his crimes.

But deep inside, Trump knows ... this is not like his reality shows
       because the Government is after his ass,
his entire circle is telling it all ... trying hard to cut off his balls
       now he understands when shit come at you fast.

He still got people wiping his behind ... patting him on his back, and telling him
that everything is going to be fine
       but you need to keep that mouth closed,
that he can't do ... he enjoy talking about the lies he thinks are true
       from the stealing of the election to the women he call 'hoes'.

Mostly all he ever talk about is his humiliation ... violence and retaliation
    of those who don't take his side
to end his disgust ... Trumps' mentality need to be thrown under the bus
    then take him for a jail house ride.

Hargis
6/27/23

EVIL IN AMERICA...
(AND ITS' GOAL)

Evil in America is still active ... it disguises itself to become more attractive
      like the NRA,
it, also, look like that woman with nothing on ... but super tight pants and a
thong
      that make even the preacher man forget to pray.

Evil in America is in that woman in the street ... lying and hustling so her
children can eat
      sarcifing her body and her health,
her babies daddy(s) are away ... because they refused to pay
      they didn't understand the connection between sex and wealth.

Evil in America is in the House and the Senate ... who haven't given it a thought
to stopping gun shooting for a minute
      and won't introduce a 'Gun Bill',
evil is the jury that said not guilty to rape ... to a man who's mind is filled hate
      and believe he can do it at will.

Evil in America us in our school ... teaching our children all the evil rules
      then watch them choke with the desire to have,
evil is smooth and slick ... evil is in the minds of the poor and the rich
      evil is in the subway with a knife, looking for someone to stab.
This is something you may not like to hear ... but it is crystal clear
      that evil is rooted in America's foundation,
everybody is doing something wrong ... drugs, shooting, or fucking Mrs. Jones
      and lying to each other about their relation.

Evil in America is in finance ... waving a few dollars to watch the black man
dance
      while smiling and rubbing his head,

he can jump high and run fast … some talk tough but (for money) are willing
to kiss ass
   and dress themselves in the bullshit they are fed.

Evil in America is in complete control … of the young and the old
   and those that think they've got it made,
evil is practiced in every State … some talk about love but are teaching hate
   but evil's goal is to put you, Democracy, and your love of God in a grave.

"The people must be free"

Hargis
5/28/23

DO YOU CARE?

Only in America do you hear about shit like this … camp Lejeune, the Monkey Pox, and shooters that never miss
> *everyday of the week,*
the Government is doing their part … by raising the price of oil
> *and inflation is making it hard for some people to eat.*

There are people who are trying to get a new bill passed … cause their son thinks he is a girl and is constantly been harassed
> *now he wants to sit instead of standing to pee,*
health care services are hard to get … politicians involvement is putting their kids life at risk
> *but they are human beings and deserves some equality.*

People are still killing people at an alarming rate … in every City, in every State
> *it doesn't look like its going to end,*
New York has created a 'no gun zone' … but that doesn't take guns out of people homes
> *so that the deranged won't kill again.*

After 60 years, Camp Lejeune is now talking about the water waste … if you were born or
live on or around the military base
> *drinking the water have caused birth defects, heart attacks, cancer, and death,*
so many people have gotten sick and didn't know why … because the City and the
State of North Carolina stuck to the same lie
> *they claimed they didn't know what was causing the people to have bad health.*

Now they want to throw out a few dollars … to keep people from hollowing
> *about their family condition,*

you know that their hearts ain't real ... so they set up this deal
      thinking that money will help solve the issue.

Doors are still getting kicked in ... by the policemen who are suppose to be your friends
      but they are shooting people dead if they make any move,
hands in the air ... they don't care
      that day, their life they will loose.

They had a warrant for an arrest ... a black man missed his court and his piss test
      eight policemen and a dog was on the scene,
the black man was lying in bed ... he raised up and moved his arms and head
      he got shot nine times by the police team.
      (he had no weapons)

People are still running scams and con games ... they have up graded their hustle and widen their range
      using the internet and face book
today, you have got to have a computer, a cell phone, and a credit card ... a lot of business don't take cash and that makes it hard
      and the scam (ers) know that most people are electronically hooked.

So what can you do? Or do you care? ... these questions are asked everywhere
      but most won't get involved or raise their voice,
unless they can get a few dollar bills ... to help strengthen their will
      but in a Capitalistic society, you always have a choice.

   "DO YOU CARE?"

                                                            Hargis
                                                            9/4/22

DOJ
(A MESSAGE TO YOU)

It's summer time … and the DOJ has not filed any crimes
        against the former President of the USA,
HE had things in his home … that didn't belong
        so with a search warrant, the FBI took them away.

Now some Republicans have sounded an alarm … Trump people are angry and armed
        ready to up hold wrong,
Trump has done so much shit … it has become an evils' _'hit list'_
        in jail is where he belongs.

Evil has got a grip on this land … and it is affecting every woman and man
        twisting their logic and their sight,
but Satan said in the book … if you take a look
        that he will make right look wrong and wrong look right.

Now we justify all of our wrongs … and will be the first ones to throw a stone
        because deceit is one of the devils' tool,
so the DOJ has got a choice … to take heed of the 1/6 committee and the peoples' voice
        or in the 2024, the devil will once again rule.

Hargis
8/30/22

IT'S HARD TO TELL (SOMETIMES)

The Klan use to wear white … and worked mostly at night
    until the #45th took control,
now some wear black rags … and a police badge
    and monitor all the voting polls.

They are Governors and Mayors … changes flat tires and braid hair
    and they are trying to deny our rights with a smile,
they deliver your mail … but will raise holly hell
    when true history is being taught to their child.

Some will cook your food and pump your gas … the old heads will tell you to
kiss their ass
    most of them have learned to hide their hand,
some will stand in the pit … and preach bull shit
    but today, they still think this is 'only' their land.

They still have no problems killing black folks … in stores, church, or sitting on
their throats
    and the court system still have problems in some cases,
because of this Country history … there is no mystery
    most shit is still based on races.

Racism is taught in everything we do … from shooting pool to practicing voodoo
    safety in America is at it's low,
my message in this poem … is don't be alarmed
    just be aware of everybody and everywhere you go.

Hargis
7/9/22

BLACK WOMEN
(2022)

A black woman received a Supreme Court seat ... Mitch and his boys were upset because (she) they could not defeat
    a task they tried hard to do,
the Democrats and the Republicans are still fighting for power ... in this late hour
    it's mid-term election time in two thousand and twenty two.

The Governorship race in Georgia is here once again ... most Georgians are hoping that the black woman win
    but racism and hatred have raised their their ugly heads,
a record number of people have come out to vote ... trying to change some laws and
remove that hand from around their throats
    and 'vomit up' the lies they have been fed.

There are black women kicking in doors and removing the fence ... they are Mayors,
Governors, and the United State Vice President
    they are good examples for our young girls to see,
today they don't have to be nurses and maids ... to be on center stage
    we even have black women that are Chief of Police.

Black women are raising the bar ... to let the world know who they are
    because they are tired of their children getting killed everywhere,
they have made it plain and clear ... that they have no fear
    and are reaching out to other women who really really care.

Their are men today making and passing laws about their bodies and their votes ...
and asking them to walk a step behind trying kill their hope
    but those days are long gone,

women of today are kicking ass and taking names ... they are the conductors of this
fast moving train
     they are running the Country, most men, and their homes.

In 2022 ... they are telling their view
     about America and what needs to be done,
the handcuffs are off ... while men are out playing golf
     Black women in America are shinning like the sun.

     WAKE UP BLACK MEN ... support and protect your women

Hargis
5/25/22

AMERICA
(AN UGLY STATE OF MIND)

*Trump poison has been released ... trying to destroy the republicans who voted
to get him impeached*
and the ones that won't spread his election lies,
Cheney went down ... but promised she'll be around
to stop Trump's White House ride.

Now two or three States ... are trying to deliberate
to charge him for some of the crimes he has caused,
some talk tough ... but Trump has call their bluff
cause he knows that many don't have the balls.

He was called from down below ... to destroy the black man show
I'm talking the President that preceded his time,
racism has always been a part of his life ... so says his cousin and his first wife
but in his head, he can't commit any crimes.

*He is being handled with kids gloves ... but he doesn't give a shit about the
American people or the God up above*
dictatorship is what he seeks,
don't get me wrong, Trump ain't no joke ... he has millions of people ready to go
most with minds that are very weak.

There are not afraid or shy ... they have threatened the FBI
if Trump goes to jail,
*this country mentality has fallen to a new low state ... when the leaders are
allowed to preach and practice hate*
that is making life for <u>we the people</u> a living hell.

Hargis
9/2/22

PRESIDENT BIDEN
(EVIL WILL NOT LET YOU REST)

It's January 2022...ain't nothing changed, ain't nothing new
     it's been over a year since the 'insurrection',
Congress and the DOJ are moving slow...talking about they need 'mo'
     people to interview (who tried to over turn the 2020 election.)

President Biden is on the TV making promises he can't keep...
because all of his 'bills' end up in the Senate in a defeat.
     Mitch McConnell and the Republicans refuse to help,
Trump is still in control...he has taken the Republican party soul
     and he is guiding them step by step.

Hannity and Fox news...are giving President Biden the blues
     slamming him on every turn he makes,
from the border to the Middle East...to the 'virus' deaths that won't
cease
     while pushing Trumps' lies and hate.

The CDC (for 3 years) has been asking people to wear masks...
if not the funeral and the grave will have your ass
     but disinformation has got some people turned around,
the truth is still the same...and you have no one to blame
     cause this 'virus' will put your ass under the ground.

Some say America is the best...but I have to confess
     that American is the best, where you pay more for less and less
     and you die at an early age from racism, hatred, and stress
     all because 'evil' will not let you rest.

Hargis
2/4/22

GREEDY
AMERICA BUSINESS OWNERS

We are living in a time that's crazy...jobs are available but people have
gotten lazy
>   truck drivers are needed,
food can't get hauled...prices won't fall
>   because business owners are greedy.

Supermarket shelves can't be filled...so families have to adjust their
meals
>   to keep from starving to death,
burgers are being made out of weeds...that will make you shit when
you sneeze
>   too much is bad for your health.

All of this is because everybody is seeking more money...damn the 'pie
in the sky' and the 'land of milk and honey'
>   to live in America, you got to have cash,
people thank God for waking them up...but between sleeps, they say
life sucks
>   now they are wondering how long is this madness going to last.

People outside think America is great...not understanding 'her' poverty
and hate
>   enforced the Capitalist because of the dollar bill,
schooling and education is good...but one thing has to be understood
>   that other people money (opm) will get you killed.

So you thank God for giving you breath...but man and his chemicals
will destroy your health
>   as you try to survive day by day,

on Capital Hill, all they do is fuss...but in reality, they suppose to be representing us

  now they have changed the voting 'laws' so they can stay.

When you look at the craziness of what's going on...you will see that some politicians are trying to make right seem wrong.

  That act as if they are self seated,

ships have stopped moving in the sea...Republicans are trying to destroy our democracy

  all because the owners of America business are greedy.

Hargis
10/26/21

NO JUSTICE...NO PEACE
(IT WAS SELF DEFENSE)

Well, the jury has done it again...let a murder go because of the color
of his skin
      none of this make sense,
a young man bring a gun to the streets...and shoot not one but three
      with tears in his eyes, he cried 'it was self defense'.

The judge did his part...informing the jury not to be so hard
      they deliberated for four days,
it was as if they forgot what was said...one wounded and two dead
      to some, a new 'hero' was made.

He had an AR15...a killing machine
      both brought across the State line by his mother,
he waved at the cops...a young man toting a gun was not stopped
      with a smile on his face, he didn't run for cover.

The love ones of those who are dead...can't get the Verdict out of their
head
      when and how can justice be served?
They can do a 'civil suit'...that may bring in some loot
      but for death, is that what they deserved?

A family got paid...because a policeman put their son in a grave
      so the City threw out some funds,
in New York, Mr. Aziz was freed from jail...after spending 55 years in
hell
      for a killing he never done.

"Too many times this slogan is used...as a defensive tool
there is no justice...there can't be any peace,
everyone has the right...not to give up their life
but these killings in America has got to cease."

Haegis
12/2/21

THE PEOPLE WANT TO KNOW

War in America rages on ... between the good and the bad, the weak and the
strong
        destruction is moving kind of fast,
Congressman J. Jordan and Miss Green ... are pushing everything
        making sure that the GOP keep kissing Trump's ass.

Despite four indictments, he is still kind of bossy ... the 14th Amendment says he
not allowed to hold any Public Offices
        but Congress has to enforce that rule,
so as it stand ... Trump is still their man
        many believe that Trump can't lose.

The people want to know ... how, when, and what will the GOP do to make
America grow
        and to make this Country safe to live,
can they create jobs that will pay more money ... so we can feed our family and
make our day sunny
        but a lot of the GOP are not being real.

We have more killing by guns than any Countries on this earth ...
because GOP don't care what human life is worth
        money and power are what they seek,
the GOP tried to pull a coup ... using racist groups
        but the transfer of Presidential power, we were able to keep.

Now America is in a bind ... because some (so called) leaders keep lying
        about what happened in the past,
but the people want to know ... like I said before
        what are your plans about inflation and the cost of gas?

From the GOP, all of their information ... is about retaliation
        and retributions,

Fox news and the GOP ... are always talking about impeaching President Joe B.
      but nothing abut the economy or life saving solutions.

So here we are in September of 2023 ... people are protesting and talking
about being free
        to choose to give or not to give birth,
to live in a world of reality ... to express their sexuality
        and to define their own human worth.

THE PEOPLE WANT TO KNOW

Hargis
9/3/23

AMERICA IS ON THE MOVE (FORWARD OR BACKWARD?)

Reports say that the economy (in 2023) is doing better ... there are some who believe it, others say 'that report' to them don't even matter
*   because living today is still very hard,*
you have to work two jobs ... kill, steal, and sometimes rob
*   just to keep from living in the dark.*

They say low wages are about to fly ... that means that everything else will be sky high
*   so financially the poor still have doubts,*
small business are shutting down ... because their profits can't be found
*   and stimulus money, most black business are always left out.*

Hollywood writers won't write ... until their money get right
*   air plane pilots are ready to go on a strike,*
the Supreme Court did not approve ... President Biden's 'forgiveness' for students going to school
*   in America, for money you have got to fight?*

Weather in America is the worse it has ever been ... Monks are now talking and Preachers are still teaching sin
*   all because the devil is showing his power,*
crime is high in every State... the GOP in Congress (for Trump) is trying to retaliate
*   in Americas' darkest hour.*

Texas Governor has given the order ... don't let anyone cross the border
*   he was talking about the Spanish immigrants,*
the homeless in California is a sight to see ... white people (in some States) are trying to re-write 'black history'
*   and Trump has told the GOP of Congress to impeach the current President.*

A black man was mauled ... by a police dog
        while he stood there with his hands in the air
he was no threat ... and yet
        he turned that dog a loose because about black people, he doesn't care.

A black woman filed a kidnapping report ... she ended up in an Alabama Criminal court
        where she plead guilty for filing a false crime,
false reports have been filed for years ... and some of them have gotten thousands of black people killed
        and no one, I mean no one, has ever done any time.

We have have been shot, beaten, hung, and drowned ... pulled apart by horses and dragged by moving cars on the ground
        and punished for learning how to read and write,
our black women were raped ... and still most say America is great
        for black manhood, many have given up the fight.

They say the jobless rate is low ... but the homeless statistics on those reports do not show
        nor are those who are just not able,
minimal wages are on the rise ... but to no one's surprise
        it's not enough (for poor people) to pay bills and put food on the table.

SO THE REAL QUESTION ... IS WHICH DIRECTION
        IS AMERICA HEADED???

                                                    Hargis
                                                    8/1/23

PEOPLE WITH NO SHAME

Coming from Africa, I use to wish upon a star … to find out where we are
traveling across the great sea,
I heard the cries from my people lips … from the sting of the slave masters' whip
but there was no place for us to flee.

When the ship anchored and settled … we were treated and sold like cattle
then they gave us their names,
many were raped and killed … some died from not eating meals
who (I asked) are these people with no shame?

Five hundred years have come and gone … still this land is not our home
even though we prayed that it would be,
in this land, we have no wealth … and our children are suffering the same death
as we did crossing the great sea.

Now we pray to and preach the words of their God … who has allowed millions
to sleep on the streets and starve
and a promise of eternal life when he returns,
but today, I can still hear the cries from my peoples' lips … from the sting of the
slave masters' whip
and I can still fell and see the hurt from the burns.

WHO (I STILL ASK) ARE THESE PEOPLE WITH NO SHAME?

Hargis
7/14/23

JUNETENTH (JUNETEEN)

Juneteen ... what does that mean?
> *a holiday for black people to celebrate*
a time when slaves were set free ... when, where, and what time was that to be
> *and who did the asking for our sake?*

Was it Lincoln, Kennedy, Obama, or Trump ... was it our blues, jazz, or James Browns' funk
> *that struck a nerve in this mentality,*
because ten years ago ... this was a no no
> *and there was no campaign for this reality.*

The Emancipation was signed over 150years ago ... and Juneteen was not a part of that show
> *so how did we get to this place and time,*
holidays were designed for business to do well ... in hope that the stock market profits will sail
> *while keeping the mentality of the masses in the blind.*

Enjoying the holidays, we sometimes forget about the homeless that have no place to sleep ... and those that are killed by gun caring creeps
> *sometime we forget about those who die of bad health,*
Juneteen ... what does that really mean
> *because the slave master mentality is still bringing about our death.*

THE SLAVES WERE SET FREE ... FROM WHO AND WHAT???

"just a little something to put on your mind"

Hargis
6/19/23

THE DEVILS' ACCOMPLISHMENTS

Ukraine is falling ... America is stalling
    world leadership is unknown,
Korea is still testing ... China is investing
    in Countries close yo home.

Biden is ignoring the signs ... concentration on trying to find
    solutions for the problems within,
but there are people on both sides of the isles ... working hard to cramp his style
    because their minds are filled with sin.

In Russia they tried to pull a coup ... they want a leadership that is new
    because Putin time has passed,
his own troops did an about face ... marching to Moscow to take over the place
    they were stopped when Putin decided to kiss ass.

In America, evil is fighting for his rights ... to bring about confusion, destruction,
and to block out light
    so that the truth can not be told or seen,
but the devil is on trial ... and some mentalities have gone wild
    trying to destroy the constitution and the American dream.

There are marching, protesting, and shooting everyday ... distrust, and death
have become the American way
    and there is no safe place to be,
the devils' angels are constantly spreading fear ... through out this land we used
to love so dear
    from sea to shinning sea.

Hargis
6/29/23

YOU CAN BE WHO YOU WANT TO BE

When you are pulled from your mothers' womb ... (some call it the tomb)
    to enter into this world,
the doctors wipe you clean ... then smack your ass to make you scream
    then check to see if you are a boy or a girl.

In America today ... some people want to change their way
    some men want to be women and some women want yo be men
the Supreme Court has changed the rules ... telling them that it's cool
    and that homosexuality is not a sin.

Homosexuality has been around for thousands of years ... King James was one
and that's for real
    and he made many think he talked with God,
he authorized the writing of this book ... that has gotten most of the world hooked
    and no one question it, ain't that odd.

That community has become powerful and brave ... they (yearly) have the 'pride
parade'
    where they march in the streets in various cities,
I have to admit ... that you have to check to see if your man or your woman is
legit
    before you lick the that penis or suck them tits.

Now I'm not trying to be disrespectful or funny ... but you have to be careful
who call honey
    because Wilhelmina may be Willie,
and insulting their rights ... you might have to fight
    to keep your ass from getting beat silly.

In Florida, you can't say gay ... because most of the Government people are
that way
    but they are all human beings
my warning to you ... is do what you got to do
    but the bible say that homosexuality is a sin.

Hargis
5/30/23

EJ VS DJ
(RAPE, SEXUAL ABUSE, AND OTHER)

Donald J … is trying to fight his way
out of law suits and possible jail time,
but he can't escape …the charges of rape
he is saying E Jean is lying.

Other ladies are telling their stories … washing away Donald J's glory
about everything is just a political plot,
he claims the DA in New York State … is filled with Donald J hate
and his run for President, he and the Democrats are trying to stop.

He says the suit is not right … because E Jean is not his type
so he won't even participate in the trial,
his lawyers had no defense … but they tried to discredit the evidence
and wanted to know why wasn't a rape report filed.

The judge and the jury wanted to know why? … Donald J didn't want to testify
and face his accuser,
the judge gave him extra time … to make up his mind
to come in and prove that he is not a woman abuser.

The jury was sent to deliberate … the former President fate
three hours is all it took,
they believed that Donald J was lying … when he said she was not his kind
they found him guilty and now it's officially in the history books.

They said Donald J should pay … 5 millions for that day
that he took away E Jeans' sexual rights,
now Donald J is looking for a deal … and talking about appeal
the formal President and his lawyers have no legal fight.

Hargis
5/8/23

IF YOU SEE SOMETHING ... SAY SOMETHING BUT....

How can you see ... when schools won't teach true history

What can you say ... when your voice (through the vote) is taken away

How can you talk ... when death and destruction is what this Country is all about

How can you see ... when your mind is closed to reality and your way of life is filled with hypocrisy

In Tennessee ... death in a school is what we see
the removal of guns was sounded by three ... now their jobs are no longer be

Racism and greed have upgraded their act ... keeping poor people poor and lynching out spoken blacks

How can you see ... when some are trying to move time back to what it use to be and your only education was a 'slave master degree'

IF YOU SEE SOMETHING ... SAY SOMETHING
BUT

What can you say ... when society has made you their prey
for not doing things their way
and fear is being taught in every State
under the banner of 'Making American Great ...again'.

Hargis
4/8/23

HOW SOON WE FORGET

Foreigners are trying their best … to come to America and rest
        and try to create a better life,
they are taking a big risk … through unknown waters and pushing back on
those who don't think they should exist
        men with their children and their wife.

White America should remember … back in the day when they crossed the great
oceans to assemble
        in someone else land,
they stole, cheated, and killed … enslaved others and made them build
        then claimed this country for the white man.

Now they don't want others to come in … unless they are Politicians' kiss ass
friends
        some say that the Mexican people are bringing in drugs and diseases,
but up north, the Canadians are crossing the border's lines … no one thinks that
it's a crime
        and getting American citizenship with ease.

Texas use to be Mexican soil … that was rich with oil
        until America killed them and took it away,
but now white America is trying to forget … all the true historical shit
        and this history, they refuse to teach their children today.

Truth is something you can't hide … and true history can't be denied
        even though some are trying to rewrite the story,
half of the truth is a lie … but evil is not shy
        his objective is to take away other's glory.

The borders up north is different than the borders down south ... when
it comes to entering this house
>   *because racism has a strong, strong hand,*
our educational hosts ... has made us believe that we are better or worst than most
>   *they have taken away some books and now they don't want others to*
>   *buy land.*

Hargis
5/14/23

"LISTEN UP"

In this land ... they say the law is equal to every man
      but 'we the people' know that's not true,
the black and the brown ... are hung and shot down
      for many, justice is long over due.

For those that got money and power ... they have their hour
      but they think they are above the law,
some have the DOJ ... turn away
      pretending they didn't see what they saw.

Trump has committed all kinds of crimes ... in this day and time
      he is still walking the streets and talking loud,
New York, Georgia, and DC ... are waiting to see
      who will be the first to bring him to trial.

On January 6th, six people died and many have been jailed ... all because
Trump told them to go and fight 'like hell',
      to stop the peaceful transformation process,
they knocked out windows and climbed the walls ... over took security and shit
in the hall
      but the transformation was still a success.

The Republicans have control of the House ... the Speaker is a shameful mouse
      he had to kiss ass to get enough votes,
now he has to bow to their will ... and all the evil deals
      to kill the people's hope.

Trump has revealed his plans ... to cause discontent and distrust all across this
land
      his mind is filled with sin,
his people have 'big balls' ... and are changing voting laws
      trying to make sure in 2024 that he win.

But God is just ... he will clear the dust
        so that you and I will be able to see,
that we have to continue to fight ... for human rights
        or 'we the people' won't be free.

Hargis
3/10/23

VOTING
(2022)

Mid – term elections in 2022 … Politicians are spending millions upon millions
of dollars
trying to get a vote from me and you
      just for the month of November,
they make promises of old … you know how the story goes
      but here is something you must always remember.

Democracy, in this land … wasn't meant for the black and brown man
      now we are fighting to keep that mentality in charge,
black and white candidates wants our votes … to hit that 'vain' of power as if we
were their dope
      getting them high and pumping up their financial heart.

So now they say anything they want … because lying to us don't really count
      because we don't have no real unity,
this party or the other … don't change our condition any farther
      neither one cares about our humanity.

Some say we are doing better … I'm talking about those who got that cheddar
      to the young, I'm talking about money,
we still live in the worst part of town …. the city use our community as a dumping
ground
      and most of our powerful black men and women have non – blacks as
      their honey.

They make us choose a side … both parties are telling us lies
      about what they can or can't do,
regardless of what you see or what you have read …it's power and money that's
in their head
      this poem is for 'we the people who are darker that blue'.

You can't forget from which you came … if you do you have only yourself to blame
 because 'evil' uses money, voting, and TV,
we will line up to vote on the 8ᵗʰ of next week … line up at the poles like we
are sheep
 but voting won't stop the killing of blacks nor will it set us free.

Hargis
11/02/22

IT'S NOT THAT HARD TO UNDERSTAND

In America no one is immune from doing wrong ... the President, the Governor,
the police all of this have been shown
       and the people have cried for their heads,
but in the last few years ... sport figures have entered into this field
       but all society has asked for is their bread.

In Atlanta, they got Vic for some dogs ... in San Francisco, Kaepernick was
protesting all
       of the killings (by the police) in this land,
in Mississippi, there was a well-fare scheme ... by the Governor and Favre to
built a volley ball court for his daughters' team
       but all they can say about Favre is that he is such a nice man.

A basketball team owner and a coach got suspended in the NBA ... one for
calling players niggas, the other they wouldn't say
       there is always two out-comes depending on the color of your face,
society wants you to think that it's not true ... and that crime is a crime and they
don't care if you are red, white, or blue
       but deep in the foundation of America is religion, money, and race.

So the black player lost their jobs and some went to jail ... some tried to appeal
but that failed
       because owners still look upon black players as slaves,
Brett Favre, also, got a million to make a speech ... an event he did not keep
       but no one was out raged.

The point that I'm trying to make ... is that everybody make mistakes
       but the difference is money and the color of your skin,
society wants us to think ... that we are all in one link
       but in America, black players have not and can not win.

Look at OJ ... the jury said for murder 'no way'
        and set him free,
but he still got 33 years ... for taking back shit that was his
        now his name in football history will never be what it should be.

Hargis
9/24/22

WAIT FOR IT
(IT'S COMING)

A 911 call, got a black man killed … he was order to stop but he refused to yield
    even though he hadn't committed a crime and didn't have a gun,
he was shot from behind … several times
    in America, all a black man can do is run.

He could have stood there with his hands in the air … but some policemen don't
care
    when it comes to blacks, they just love pulling the trigger,
the Grand Jury won't indict … when told of the policeman fright
    this is America and (and to them)he's just a nigga.

One of these days and it won't be long … the police and the Grand Jury will
be in a 'trouble zone'
    then they will be talking about 'black love',
they'll all be mad … cause they think they have to kiss black people ass
    and pray to the black God up above.

Malcolm said "an eye for an eye" … for those who think that the bible don't lie
    you know that God didn't turn the other cheek,
he really got down … sent forth bad weather, bees, and some he drown
    he wanted the dis – believers to know that he wasn't weak.

Jesus was a black man … who grew up in Egypt (Africa)land
    he talked about loving your enemy like you love yourself,
the people felt the loss … when he was nailed to a cross
    betrayed by Judus for a little bit of wealth.

White people have been killing black people for hundreds of years …
    prosecution they never feared
    because their Constitution said that people was not human beings
some of the laws have changed … and the Grand Jury still won't blame
    most of them for these killing sins.

Black day is coming, black day is near ... when America will be faced with this internal fear
  by Gods' children who won't turn the other cheek,
it will be a new generation ...that will have no hesitation
    because it's redemption for our spilled blood they seek.

Hargis
9/6/22

MONKEY POX
(A NEW KID ON THE BLOCK)

The corona virus had our backs against the rocks … now they some shit they
call 'the Monkey Pots'
      that is spreading through the USA,
but when you got men marrying men … the book says that's a sin
      not a word from the Christian leaders of today.

People say that God loves everybody (we know that's a lie) … because those that
are against him (he make sure that they die)
      I'm talking about ministers, pastors, and Imam the same,
man and woman were created for each other … but man has taken it a step farther
      now we wonder why do many people are deranged.

Evil is dressed to kill … and forcing on people its' will
      it is really in control,
from the food that you eat … to the future that you seek
      it has your will power and your soul.

This Monkey Pot they say … comes from the Africa way
      cause man and monkeys were having sex,
sounds like a modern form of aids … but on a higher stage
      it took years before we found out that the information was incorrect.

First there were gonorrhea and aids … so having sex, most people were afraid
      because too many ended up dead,
now this Monkey Pox will bring about some deaths … so once again we have
to be careful with our sex health
      but still, "bull shit", <u>we the people</u> are still been feed.

Hargis
9/1/22

RESPECT AND HOPE

In the UK ... the Prime Minister walked away
       accursed of many crimes,
in Japan, during a campaign ... the former Prime Minister was shot with no shame
       with a (home made gun) from behind.

In Japan, very few people have guns ... the gun killing rate is almost none
       the whole Country in in shock,
so it doesn't matter where you live ... a kill is a kill
       and killing is something that no one can stop.

In America, another mass shooting took place ... during a 4th of July parade
       38 shot, 7 dead,
he pulled the trigger seventy times ... then drank a glass of wine
       21 years old, what was in his head.

America (we know) is the center of the earth ... but it did not give evil its' birth
       America just nursed it and made it strong,
the devil is here ... and is spitting out nothing but fear
       but over 70 millions Americans don't think he is wrong.

Every year in America, thousands are laid to rest ... taking some one's life is what
America does best
       in every Town and every State,
those in charge speak about sorry and pain ... in front of a camera, they always
have someone else to blame
       but they allow some people to practice hate.

Former Prime Minister Abe ... the people of Japan will no longer see
       they will honor him in the next few days,
President Biden will show his respect .. his sorry and his regrets
       but hoping that our Japan / America relationship doesn't fade.

Hargis
7/8/22

THE 4TH OF JULY
(INDEPENDENCE DAY)

This is a day of celebration … all across this Nation
        fire works will light up the sky,
it's freedom for most … I'm talking about (the so-called) host
        but because of 'mass killings', a lot of families will sit and cry.

2022 is the year … for cooking burgers, hot dogs, and drinking beer
        people are traveling from State to State,
how soon we forget … about all the other shit
        that allow some people to practice hate.

The Supreme Court think they got big balls … so they changed some laws
        that got people upset, marching, and singing songs,
independence day … that's what they say
        but the changing of some 'laws' are just wrong.

This is the 4ᵗʰ of July … and some people will die
        because evil don't take a break,
so be mindful of the time … and watch your behind
        everywhere you go, your life is at stake.

HAPPY 4ᵗʰ OF JULY

Hargis
7/4/22

BEWARE

Summer is here ... the days are bright and clear
   children are seeking fun, fun, fun
parents are wondering what to do ... working and keeping up with their kids too
   the heat is on and Mr. evil is looking for your daughter and your son.

The lake area is filled with unsuspected minds ...fishing and bar-b-Q(ing)having
a good time
   families enjoying families (what could go wrong?)
hand shakes, laughter, and hugs ... can beer, soda pops, and drugs
   and the music is always somebody's favorite song.

Then Mr. evil and Miss ugly just happen to pop in ...some know them and call
them friends
   but this is the season when they run wild,
they will eat your food ... and you start thinking they are cool
   but when night comes, someone is missing a child.

Evil and ugly look like me and you ... they live in the minds of unsuspected crew
   so be mindful of everyone around,
empty minds and summer heat ... that's a combination that can't be beat
   evil and ugly will turn your summer smile into a seasonal frown.

BEWARE BEWARE BEWARE

Hargis
7/1/22

LOCK HIM UP
(THAT'S THE WILL OF THE PEOPLE)

I turned on the tube … to watch the news
        about the January 6th insurrection,
in this trial …which is kind of wild
        is all about Trump lies of the 2020 election.

He started in January of that year … putting in the minds of his people (some fear)
        about if he loose, the election is rigged,
if you tell a lie enough … people will begin to believe that stuff
        then they (the people) will do his bid.

Some Senators and Fox news say that the insurrection was just a fake …
even though they got it on tape
        and some people were killed,
Trump created the whole scene … because the loss made him mean
        the Proud boys, the Oath keepers, and others said they were doing
        Trump's will.

Trump pass out Gorilla glue … for those who
        wanted to stick to kissing his ass,
miss Green, Ted, and Mitch … Trump's Senators bitch
        got a double dose, trying to make it last.

The testimonies were a lot … Barr and Trump's daughter tried get Trump to stop
        but Trump was in his 'fuck you' mind state,
most was convinced … that Trump wanted to hang Mike Pence
        so Pence called in the troops before it got too late.

Democrats and Republicans had to run and hide ... all because Trump lied
    and directed them to fight like hell,
he wanted to stay in power ... by destructing the votes in that hour
    this trial should end with Trump in jail.

Hargis
6/9/22

HAPPY BLACK HISTORY MONTH
(2022)

February 2022...the only month that blacks are allowed to boast about what they use to do
> I guess black history is only 28 days long,

for five hundred years...we were claimed, renamed, contained, and framed with fears
> we use to be Muhammad and Kenyatta, now we are Smith and Jones.

We watch (so called) black movies all month long...did you know that 'BET' was 'WHITE' owned?
> And our history did not start with us being slaves,

with our sweat and blood, we helped build this land...that was taken from the Red and Brown man
> that effort put millions in their graves.

Today (at this time)...they are trying to make 'true' history a crime
> by removing and burning books,

but there is always a few blacks...that keep speaking the facts
> and reminding us of the effort it took.

The shortest month of the year...white folks allow us to celebrate and cheer
> about our contributions in building this house

they don't want us to talk about the killings, the burnings, and the destruction of our homes...nor about the disrespect because to them black men was never 'grown'
> in the North, East, West, and South.

While we are celebrating...they are calculating
> new ways of beating our flesh to the bone,

by making some famous...you know like Andy and Amos
> who will stand and say "that the white man has done no wrong".

You can see them on 'Fox news'...talking like fools
    trying to avoid the sting of the 'slave master' whip',
they have the language down pat...but their message is 'not' 100% facts
    but it keeps from being in the hull of the slave ship.

Now they focus on their money, their homes, and their cars...his
education that will make them 'super stars'
    so our youth will be easier to control,
the mentality that owned the plantations...is the same mentality that run
and own this nation
    but their efforts will never stop our history from been told.

HAPPY BLACK HISTORY MONTH

Hargis
2/11/22

GOOD-BY 2021

Hoo-weee...let me see
     a lot of shit happened in this year,
politicians were corrupted...crime rates were up
     and killings kept family members in tears.

President Biden brought the troops home...Republicans say he was wrong
     but this ended a 20 year war,
he gave praise to the women and men...and honored those who we will never see again
     to many families, he brought back 'joy'.

Trump and his crew...tried to pull a coup
     by storming Capital Hill,
most of the country was shocked...the transfer of power, he tried to stop
     many were injured and many were killed.

Joe Manchin got the Democrats by the balls...he won't help the people at all
     many think he is pushing for a higher spot,
Democracy is been torn apart...but he doesn't feel it in his heart
     he is an undercover Republican for 'FOX'.

The virus has doubled down...still killing people in every city and every town
     and still many won't take the shots or wear the masks,
some business (again) had to close...the jobless rate rose
     so did the food and the gas.

In Chicago, the story is been told...that the Black Mayor has no control
     because so many people (this year) have been killed,
in Texas, the Governor said...this new 'law' get it in your head
     then he signed the 'abortion' bill.

"THE SUPREME COURT" DIDN'T TAKE A STAND…
NOW STATES ARE DOING IT ALL OVER THE LAND.
AMERICA IS FALLING APART.

President Biden is trying to do right…but evil is putting up a bigger fight
    Republicans are beating on their chest,
Trump has sewed his seeds…and they have grown indeed
    because with evil, there can be no rest.

Mother nature was doing her thing…tornadoes, storms, and, hurricanes
    reeking habit through out the South,
out West, there were fires and looting…gang violence and drive-by shootings
    and a black Republican (DJ) ran for Governor of the house.

In sports, the virus made it's play…taking down players and almost stopping the 'NBA'
    but the games must go on,
with the virus, you can't play ball…that put some teams up against the wall
    no masks, no shots…the same old song.

This year will end in a couple of weeks…you need to thank God for this treat
    for you being above ground,
you think that 2021 was bad…2022 is gonna make you mad
    just pray that this time next year you are still around.

"may the peace and blessings of God be upon you"

Hargis
12/22/21

MARCH NO MORE
(THE GHETTO PROPHESY)

The killing of black people has not changed ... five hundred years, no one to blame
     and society just moves on,
sometimes (so called leaders) cry out loud ... and may draw a 'black lives matter' crowd
     but all they do is just march and sing songs.

One day, one will rise up and won't be shy ... his motto will be 'an eye for an eye'
     that will put some killings in check,
his followers will be so large ... there will be no need for songs or march
     because they will bring about: peace, comfort, and respect.

Laws will be changed and removed from the Constitution ... Congress will be working together to fine solutions
     and the Supreme Court will really be Supreme,
there will still be some holding on to destruction and hate ...
spreading misinformation on how to make America great
     because there will be no such thing as the 'white American dream'

This was prophesied many years back ... that have led to the killing of millions of blacks
     but the time is near,
this force will not be stopped by birth control or grave yards ... nor by the evil/ugly mentality that hides in the dark
     people will love people and not live in fear.

Hoover thought it was King ... but realized that he only had a dream
     so he tried to destroy every black organization,

but he didn't live in the hood ... so he misunderstood
     the power of a 'unified' people across this nation.

"The people must be free"

Hargis
8/12/2020

THE AMERICAN DREAM

The American dream ... it may seem
     like your pie in the sky,
but the meaning has been lost ... destroyed by the crime boss
     a lot of dreamers do noting but cry.

The American dream use to be a goal ... for immigrants and people not so old
     but bad economic and high taxes changed those thoughts,
no jobs ... and the Country being run by the mob
     people are now wondering what is America all about?

Mass shootings and the rathe of God ... no gun laws and nothing has been solved
     racism and hatred is on the rise,
an unknown virus all over the world ... is killing men, women, boys, and girls
     and our President keep telling us lies.

Still some dream of the house with the picket fence ... two children and good job
that will pay the rent
     while many have no place to live,
profits for the rich is very high ... they pay no taxes and some are wondering why?
     They always take and never give.

Yes, the American dream ... it may seem
     that it's your pie in the sky,
while it keeps you dreaming ... the rich keep scheming
     and a lot of dreamers will continue to cry.

Hargis
5/01/2019

RUSSIA...UKRAINE
NATO

It is March 2022 ... in my life, there is nothing new
>   but in the world, there is a war going on,
Russia has invaded another land ... the US and NATO are forced to take a stand
>   sanction is name of their song.

Fox news is still up holding Trump ... while still kicking President Biden in the rump
>   reporting what Trump said 'back' when,
people are dying and Ukraine need some assistance ... because Russia is moving
through their Country with hardly no resistance
>   world leaders are watching (some with a shitty grin).

>   NATO voted and said that Putin is wrong ... but the killing of people is still going on
>   the people in Russia are protesting for Putin to stop,
NATO has sanctioned Putin oil and money ... but his tanks and jets keep coming
>   Putin wants to turn Ukraine into a parking lot.

Millions of people have had to flee ... before Putin take over their city
>   and it seems like it's just a matter of time,
some (US) Republicans and 4 other countries said Putin is right ...
but NATO said they will 'not' join the fight
>   they are charging Putin with war crimes.

Complete destruction and it won't be long ... Ukraine as we know it will soon be gone
>   the US and NATO are seen as being weak,

the US and NATO are just tools ... this Ukraine and Russia war is
being misconstrued

there is another agenda that someone else seeks.

I wouldn't be surprised if Trump had a hand ... in Putin sudden
invasion of this land

because Ukraine would not succumb to his will,
Americans are drinking, partying, and having fun ... watching the
news and old movies reruns

while Ukraine people are being killed.

"EVIL STILL RULES THE WORLD"

Hargis
3/5/22

AMERICA, AMERICA

America America: do you hear what I hear ...
                   the masses of your people are living in fear
                             of gangs, racism, and Government too,
                   afraid to get stopped ... by a crooked cop
                       or dragged off a plane by the airport crew.

America America: can you hear the people cry ...
                   life is getting worse and they want to know why
                             and why you think drugs are the answer to all things,
                   from birth to death ... you have fucked with their health
                             keeping them sleep and thinking about dreams.

America America: the people are trying to understand ...
                   how did the 'ugly mentality' get control of this land
                             and set up shop in every State,
                   stealing their wills ... through crooked deals
                             and intensifying their abilities to hate.

America America: you were once 'the land of the free' ...
                   understood and loved from sea to shinning sea
                             before 'profit' raised her head,
                   now people are bold ... and out of control
                             and for that money they will shoot you dead.

America America: what are you going to do ...
                   to ensure that your future will be true
                       because the whole world is now watching you.

Hargis
4/28/17

OH SAY ... CAN'T YOU SEE?

There were some people that got killed ... in a military drill
  their plane was blown from the sky,
thirty people they say ... have seen their last day
  now their families and friends can do nothing but cry.

In another part of the world ... a gunman killed men, women, boys, and girls
  he said "it was in the name of Christ",
a Muslim talked about his God ... and beaten by a mob
  they said "feared for their life".

A mother drowned four of her kids ... and said "that God approved of what
she did"
  then the State allowed her to adopt more,
in 'sippi' no one even hollered ... when two little black girls was put in jail for
stealing twelve dollars
  they got "LIFE" because they were black and poor.

Then there was the case where a baby was drowned ... duck taped and missing
thirty days before found
  the mother was only found guilty for telling a lie,
when they let her go ... most people shouted "NO NO NO"
  black folks who watched just said "oh my".

The Government allowed some States ... to exercise their hate
  with laws to put and keep Mexicans out,
but they are letting men marry men ... ain't that a sin?
  So what is being an American all about?.

Preachers and priests are still doing their 'thane' ... taking advantage of women
and little children (oh what a shame)
  all because of an education that won't let them see,
beyond paying bills ... and hustling for a meal
  this pressure (called life) just won't let you be.

They gave Vic time for some dogs … a mother drown her baby 'get nothing at all'
     I guess 'the dog' is mans' best friend,
Madoff took billions in cash … then told the world to kiss his ass
     now he is living a luxurious life in the pen.

A Congress woman got shot in the head … and was left in the store for dead
     everyday people cried and prayed,
but six other people were slain … no one even know their names
     with them, the Capitalist can't get paid.

The stock market is falling like rain … the rich are going insane
     two thousand interviewed for ten jobs this week,
the wealthy sit back and laugh … while their profit grow fast
     people die everyday cause they can't eat.

In England, Africa, and Asia too … people are protesting against being controlled by a few
     the world news is asking the leadership to step down,
the United Nation have gotten involved … bum rushing other countries like the mob
     and the Humanitarians of the world ain't made a sound.

Where are the preachers of peace … and the world police?
     I guess all truths won't see you free,
so the question is still the same … who do you blame?
     For an education that won't let you see.

Hargis
8/19/11

SPEAKER OF THE HOUSE
(THE CHAIR IS VACANT)

GOP *can't seem to get enough votes … to crown a Speakers' hope*
       Jim J. wanted the job,
he was recommended by Donald J … but twenty two Republicans said no way
       because Jim was involved with the 'insurrection mod'.

Congress is still in disarray … no Speaker of the House as of this day
       so no legislation or bill can be passed,
this situation President Biden can't accept … because the USA allies are in need
of America's help
       but no one knows how long this is going to last.

With no Speaker, America is in a bad spot … can't give aid to Israel or stop
Russia from making Ukraine a parking lot
       man hatred for man is everywhere,
in this hour … no one man should have absolute power
       he will destroy humanity and won't even care.

The GOP who is elected as the Speaker of the House … should be a
Representative with vision and not that of a mouse
       and who will work with both sides of the isle,
the Speakers' job is no treat … because the Government is scheduled to shut
down in a few weeks
       he has to ignore that special crowd who are just talking loud.

Making promising to get votes … that special crowd will have you by your throat
       and make you look weak as shit,
and when they have had enough … they will throw you under the bus
       then put you on Donald J's hit list.

At the rate we are going … America will be torn
*   apart very soon,*
Democracy will be lost … the President (once again) will be the crime boss
*   then retributions, lying, and deceit will be Americas' doom.*

THE CHAIR IS STILL VACANT

Hargis
10/19/23

GEORGIA
(SWEET, SWEET GEORGIA)

Breaking news … another one has decided to choose
        to plea guilty to a Georgia crime,
it doesn't look good for Donald J … who is use to having his way
        they all are saying that he was lying.

Some are beginning to sing like birds … saying stuff that was never heard
        to keep from going to jail,
DA Willis ain't sparing no blows … she is after white men, niggas, and ho(s)
        who were trying to get the Georgia election to fail.

The prize is the top dog … who mad that historical phone call
        asking for over 11,000 more votes,
then he sent down his gang … who he had trained
        to over throw the Georgia peoples' hope.

Rudy G and the crew … thought they knew what to do
        when it comes to southern folks,
but to their surprise … Georgia was already aware of Donald J lies
        so Georgia pull the old 'rope-dope'.

DA Willis brought forth the Rico Act … and indicted 19 to be exact
        and some thought that she had lost her mind,
19 in a trial … that would be kind of wild
        but in Georgia, the sun does shine.

Five have already flipped … because they didn't want to take that prison trip
        and more is on the way,
the Georgia GOP tried to get her to go … but the GOP Governor told them
'hell no'
        he said DA Willis and this trial are going to stay.

Now here we are in October of 23 ... the Country can now see
what an evil mentality will try,
he doesn't care who gets hurt ... or who suffers or bite the dirt
he just want you and me to believe the big lie.
So he can tell Democracy and Biden bye bye.

Hargis
10/25/23

150 YEARS
OF PROCESSING

1863 is the year ... "Mr. President, we have blocked all avenues of light to the slaves mind"

> *"you can now sign the proclamation papers to make them think they are"*
> *"free"*

To control the slave thoughts (during and after slavery), they were introduced to Unimaginable fears:

> *KKK*
> *Racism*
> *Lack of educational*
> *Hanging*
> *No voting rights*

To control their emotions, they were introduced to the bible:

> *Test ... the killing of Martin Luther King Jr.*
> *Reactions ... rioting and burning all over the Country*
> *Solution ... Capitalism and materialism*

To break up the black family and to destroy any type of black unity, they were introduced to birth control pills, drugs, self destruction

> *Test ... the beating of Rodney King*
> *Reaction ... rioting, burning, and stealing*
> *Solution ... more Capitalism, more drugs, Movies, and a black President*

To destroy any future leadership within the black community, they were introduced to
gang violence, imprisonment, and death to black youth

> *Test ... Tray Martin*
> *Reaction ... black people took into consideration their homes, cars, jobs*

friends, and images
Solution ... ?????

PROCESS COMPLETE

Mr President, "we have successfully blocked all avenues to the slaves mind
"but just in case, we have Al and Jessie standing by"

Hargis
7/14/13

WHY? WHY? WHY?

In Cali another shooting...in Florida, people are rooting
      because the "Tray Martin" trial is about to begin,
in Boston, a terrorist raised his head...an explosion that left may dead
      in America, it's not news unless it's a sin.

In DC, the 'shit' is still there...the people now know that Congress
don't care
      they feel that their representative has left them all alone,
the NSA...is listening to what you say
      in your house and on your cell phones.

In Oklahoma, tornadoes have torn the place up...the Governor shouted
"what the fuck"
      am I and this state going to do,
the people have come to understand...that 'Home Land Security' ain't
the plan
      other cities have put together their own helping crew.

In New York City...life is never pretty
      gangs are snatching cell phones,
in the South, it's a different mind...people are praising Jesus and
committing crimes
      America America an education gone wrong.

The economy they say is looking good...not in my hood
      gangs, drugs, and killings still rule the streets,
technology has taken away life's surprise...because everything is now
computerized
      from job hunting, to dating, to the cooking of your meat.

The dollar use to be back up by gold...but the 'super rich' got that under
control
      now a dollar ain't hardly worth shit,

but 'we the people' work hard all week...it's that pay check we seek
       then turn around and give most of it back to rich.

Business(s) plot day and night...to keep from your mind any 'light'
       that will allow you to keep your cash,
because of our education in 'greed'...and the 'desires' that they feed
       we fall for the scams, the promises, and the ideals that never last.

The younger generations are looking real hard...worrying about their start
       wondering what will be their 'ball of fire',
they are looking at the world in a different light...and see that things just ain't right
       they are asking the question: <u>WHY? WHY? WHY?</u>

Hargus
6/10/2013

THE REALITY OF NOW

Matt Gaetz is at it again ... vowed to not let power get issued to the Speaker
Pro Temp
    because his choice was Jim J.,
Jim J gave up, saying the GOP sucks
    twenty two Republicans said "Jordan, no way".

The GOP is out of control ... and their inabilities are putting the Country on
hold
    as America is being pulled into the middle-East war,
America military has made some moves ... this is in case Iran or Iraq decide to
choose
    to intervene and roar.

President Biden in calculating his decision ... asked Congress for 106 billion
    to support Israel and Ukraine,
but after three weeks, Congress can't answer the demand ... because 217 votes
are needed
    to elect a Speaker man
    the GOP has brought nothing to the House but shame, shame, shame.

Our military is in limbo ... because Senator Tuberville (the red-neck from
Alabama) is saying no, no
    to promoting top leadership,
he said, it's all about abortion, but we know he is lying ... it's about racism,
because a black man is next in line
    so this Senator is willing to sink the whole ship.

A pilot went berserk ... while at work
    6,000 feet in the air,
he was out of his mind ... for a short period of time
    he gave everybody on the plane a scare.

He said it was that 'magic mushroom' … that he consumed
        and hasn't slept in 40 hours,
his illusion was deep … because he thought he was sleep
        drugs and its' power.

If he had succeed … 83 people would have been deleted
        from the friendly skies,
so, no one can really tell … who is or not living in mental hell
        or the reasons why some has to die.

Hargis
10/23/23

IS IT SO?

You won't believe what is happening in the land of the plenty and the home of
the brave ...
white folks (today) still think they own slaves
    that they control,
when you look at the NBA ... I guess you can sort of say
    that black men are been bought and sold.

There are some that try to escape ... and some that become great
    (so called) examples for little black boys,
there are some who think they have it made... they are bought, sold and or trade
    but to white owners, they are just toys.

They use to killed black men for sport starting back in 1592 ... when white folks
(to themselves) were being true
    to who they really are,
so here today ... that mentality has not gone away
    and the killing of black men has continued so far.

A lot of this is pass down from generation to generation ... that's the real
education
    but most of the writers of black history are white,
they put black men on display ... from November to Father's day
    their masters and his money have taught them how not to fight.

So the slave – master relationship is still a team ... some talk about freedom and
a holiday called June-teen
    but the justification of black deaths has not changed,
in some cases black folks are in charge ... but they have no love for self in their
hearts
    and they kill other black men with no shame.

No you won't believe what is happening in the land of the plenty and the home
of the brave...

white folks still own plantations and still own slaves
        in 2022,
they allow some blacks to compete ... for their entertainment treat
        to keep them rich, and to themselves be true.

Now hiring ... applications are accepted on the day of the draft.
        <u>*Trained white women are standing by to help.*</u>

Hargis
6/19/22

PREDICTIONS

Some say that Trump will win ... which will be a political sin
*   for someone who has openly vowed to use his position for retributions,*
against Republicans, Democrats, blacks and whites ... all of those who refuse
to keep up his fight
*   that will be his dictatorships' solution.*

The Democrats will win the House and the Senate ... that will keep him in check
for a minute
*   but his plan for Democracy is destruction,*
he doesn't care about right or wrong ... evil is rooted in his bones
*   life in America will be restructured.*

He will do away with the electoral votes ...and restrict black and brown peoples'
hopes
*   then he will deport all Migrants or put them in jail,*
the Supreme Court will be his tool ... to legalize all of his bullshit rules
*   America will be renamed to: the United States oh Hell.*

There will be no elections, he will appoint the Governors to each State ... because
Trump thinks he is the 'only one' that can make America great
*   again and again and again,*
his running mate ... will be Matt Gaetz,
*   Jim Jordan or that bitch from Georgia who is filled with sin.*

With that been said ... the American dream will be dead
*   and you will have no one to blame,*
but your vote in 2024 ... against Trump, will close this door
*   and bring about an end to evils' game.*

Hargis
11/18/23

Printed in the United States
by Baker & Taylor Publisher Services